THE WOMAN
WHO PLEASES GOD

Fay Smart and Jean Young

Original text material by Fay Smart and Jean Young
Developed by Emmaus Correspondence School
which is an extension ministry of
Emmaus Bible College
founded in 1941.

ISBN 0-940293-37-4

567890/432

© 1977 Emmaus Bible College

Printed in the United States of America

Instructions to Students

The first responsibility of all Christians—men and women—is to find the place that God has appointed for them. We could have no higher honor than to *be* what God intended us to be and to do what He sent us to do. What *is* God's will for women? The purpose of this course is to examine what the Bible says about women so that we may—

1. Determine God's plan and purpose for women
2. Learn from example and instruction what qualities of character are pleasing to God
3. Discover the New Testament principles governing women's conduct and relationships
4. Examine the kinds of ministry open to women in the home, the church, the secular world and the mission field
5. Study spiritual gifts with a view to personal evaluation of gift and a setting of goals according to God's expectations.

The late Peter Marshall once prepared a sermon entitled, "Keeper of the Springs," in which he stressed the importance of keeping the little springs high in the hills clear and free of impurity if the flowing rivers were to be clean and pure for the blessing of mankind. In a real sense, women are "keepers of the springs," as they train and influence children and mold the characters of those who will be the leaders of the future. This awesome responsibility and privilege is shared by all women, single as well as married, and the quality of its womanhood has a real influence on a nation's morality and strength.

May God help us to find our place in His great program and, in the doing of His will, to glorify Him.

LESSONS YOU WILL STUDY

HOW TO STUDY

Begin by asking God to open your heart to receive the truths He would teach you from His Word. Read the lesson through at least twice, once to get the general drift of its contents and then again, slowly, looking up all Scripture references and examining all footnotes.

EXAMS

Each exam covers two lessons. (Exam 1, for example, covers Lessons 1 and 2.) Each exam is clearly marked to show you which questions deal with which lesson. You may take the exam in two stages. When you have completed Lesson 1, you may take the part of the Exam 1 dealing with that lesson.

You may use any version of the Bible for general study. When answering exam questions, however, restrict yourself to either the Authorized (King James) Version (1611), the New King James Version (1980), or the New American Standard Bible. These are three widely used versions. There are so many versions today that your instructor cannot possibly check them all in evaluating your work.

1. Thought and Research Questions

Some exams contain questions designed to make you do original Bible study. You may use your Bible to answer these questions. They are clearly marked.

2. What Do You Say? Questions

Questions headed in this way are optional and no point value is assigned to them. You may freely state your own opinions in answer to such questions. Your candid answers will help your instructor get to know you better as an individual. They will also help us evaluate the general effectiveness of this course.

3. How Your Papers Are Graded

Any incorrectly answered questions will be marked by your instructor. You will be referred back to the place in the Bible or the textbook where the correct answer is to be found.

PERSONAL QUESTIONS TO PONDER

After each lesson there are some personal questions to ponder. These questions are not required for examination purposes. Rather, they are intended to help you relate the truths learned in the lessons to your own life. If you wish, you may send your answers to these questions to your instructor for comment and evaluation. You will, however, probably prefer to keep these as a record of your personal response to the lessons.

A PERSONAL PRAYER

After studying each lesson and all Bible passages referred to, and answering the personal questions to ponder, in the space provided, write out your personal prayer to God. This will help you become a woman who pleases God.

FURTHER STUDY

Recommendations for further optional studies are made at the end of some lessons. These are designed to guide you into some areas for greater-in-depth studies.

MEMORY VERSE ASSIGNMENTS

Memory verse assignments are included at the end of some lessons. Make sure you learn these verses so as to be able to quote them fluently.

RECORD YOUR GRADES

When you send in your first exam a Grade Record Card will be returned to you showing your grade for the lesson(s) just corrected. You must return this card to the School each time you send in further exams.

GROUP ENROLLMENTS

If you are enrolled in a class, submit your exam papers to the leader or secretary of the class who will send them for the entire group to the Correspondence School.

TEACHER'S MANUAL

A teacher's manual for this course is available from the School for use in class situations. Write to the School for details.

GENERAL INSTRUCTIONS

Begin studying immediately, or, if you are in a group, as soon as the group begins. Try to keep a regular study schedule. Endeavor to complete one lesson each week and one exam every two weeks. This will enable you to complete the course in three months. You may prefer to complete an exam each week and the course in six weeks. However, you will be allowed a maximum of one year to complete this course from the time of enrollment.

ADVANCED COURSE

For those who successfully complete this course at "popular" level, advanced study material is available. This comprises a study guide bringing the course to "college" level. Students successfully completing the advanced series will earn two credits in the Emmaus Bible College residence program in Dubuque, Iowa. Write to the Correspondence School for details.

Created for a Purpose
(Genesis 1 and 2)

In the first chapters of Genesis we see an intelligent Creator working according to a pattern and design. "And God saw everything that He had made, and, behold, it was very good" (Gen. 1:31). He saw all that He had made functioning according to His plan—and "God ... rested" (2:2). There was order, peace and satisfaction when each part of creation was *performing that for which it was made.*

Similarly, the key to a happy and fulfilled life for us is to find out what God intended us to be, what He fitted us for, and to accept gladly the place of His appointment—to fit in with His plan. If He has a purpose for all His creatures, then He has a purpose for me. My first responsibility (and the obviously sensible thing to do) is to discover that purpose.

Our first glimpse of God's intention for women comes in Genesis 1:27, 28—"So God created man in His own image, in the image of God created He him; *male and female* created He them." Here the bisexual nature of humanity is clearly stated: both man and woman are in the image of God. "And God blessed them." The will of God for men and women has always been to bless them. Let us remember that.

"And God said unto *them,* Be fruitful and multiply, fill the earth and subdue it, and have dominion ... over every living thing...." Man and woman stand here as equals before God, one in life and work, one in nature and dominion, God's representatives on earth.

As we read on in Genesis chapter two and are given the details of the creation of mankind, the woman emerges as a distinct personality, differing from the man in significant ways. We must note the difference in the time, manner and purpose of her creation.

CREATION OF WOMAN

The Bible tells us that Adam was created *first*. "God formed man of the dust of the ground and breathed into his nostrils the breath of life (2:7) ... And the Lord God took the man and put him into the garden of Eden to dress it and to keep it ... and the Lord God said, It is not good that man should be alone" (2:15-18).

Adam, the first human, stood alone in the midst of the beauty and abundant life of the garden. And for the first time in His creation God said, "It is *not* good." Adam was a social being, made for fellowship and needing it, but in all the animal creation there was no creature that corresponded to him, nothing on his level of being (2:20). So God said, "I will make a help meet for him" (suited to him) (2:18).

God caused the man to fall into a deep sleep and took from his side bone and flesh; from these God built a woman. She was not made from the dust *(adamah)* as was the man; she was made from the man *(adam)*. She was of his very nature—bone of his bones and flesh of his flesh (2:23). Woman, the result of God's creative labor and skill, was made *for* man and *from* man and was presented to him as his counterpart and partner, his complement—that which completed him.

SIGNIFICANCE OF ORDER OF CREATION

Is there significance in the order of creation—man first, then woman? The New Testament tells us there is. Paul wrote to Timothy: "I suffer not a woman to teach, nor to usurp authority over the man, but to be in silence. *For* Adam was first formed, then Eve" (1 Timothy 2:12, 13). Dealing with the subject of headship, 1 Corinthians chapter 11 says: "... the head of the woman is the man ... For the man is not of the woman, but the woman of the man. Neither was the man created for the woman, but the woman for the man." (1 Corinthians 11:3, 8, 9).

Obviously, there is a difference in position of the one formed first, who is to be the "head," and the one formed afterwards, who is not to "usurp authority" over him. This does not lower the value, or worth, of woman as a person in God's sight. In a society of equals, one must take the leadership.

PURPOSE OF WOMAN'S CREATION

God clearly stated His purpose in creating woman. She was to be a "help" for the man. The word translated "help" has no connotation of inferiority. The same word, occurring twenty-one times in the Old Testament, is used sixteen times to speak of someone superior, often of God Himself (e.g., Genesis 49:25; Exodus 18:4). The woman was to share Adam's dignity and glory as ruler over the earth; she was to help him fill his God-appointed role (Genesis 1:28).

God Himself "brought her unto the man" (2:22) and Adam exclaimed, "This is *at last* one suitable for me!" No mention is made here of the woman as a child-bearer; she is valued for herself alone, as one who could share Adam's thoughts, speech and self-hood since she shared his very life and nature. In His wise design God created male and female. *He* put the differences there (Matthew 19:4). The sexes were to be complementary, not competitive—each contributing something to the other, able to do so because of the unique characteristics implanted by God.

While recognizing the woman's privilege and honored position, we do well to note that the stated purpose of her creation was in relation to man. She did not stand alone on the earth, related only to God. Adam was uniquely God's man; the woman was created to be Adam's "help." Made subsequent to Adam, formed from him, made for him—it was he who made life meaningful for her—yet without her, he was incomplete. She was his complement, essential to his wholeness.

The order of creation of man and woman expresses God's order of relationship and authority. The one formed first is to lead; the one formed after, and from him, is to follow and give support. The man was not created to help and be the helper for woman, but woman was created to help and be the helper for man. This is *God's* appointed order.

How does God want you to help your husband? Think this through carefully. Give him understanding support. Don't make it hard for him to be the man God wants him to be! In the church, respect and cooperate with the elders. Help them to do the work God has called them to do.

MARRIAGE

Following the creation of woman and Adam's delighted recognition of her as his true counterpart, we are given God's ideal for marriage. "Therefore shall a man leave his father and mother, and shall cleave unto his wife: and they shall be one flesh" (2:24). Marriage is the oldest human institution—established by God and intended for the welfare of society. Note that marriage is not a *Christian* institution, not a church ordinance, but was established at the very beginning of the human race; it is intended for the good of all people, regardless of religious beliefs or lack of them.

In the guidelines for marriage laid down in Genesis 2:24, the words "leave" and "cleave" stress the *exclusive* and *lifelong* character of the relationship as God intended it to be. In becoming "one flesh" the man and the woman establish a new and permanent unit in society; they leave their former relationships for this new one. Monogamy is God's plan—one man cleaving to one woman, each completing the other in every aspect of life, functioning as a unit. This is an *exclusive* relationship.

In the Gospels it is recorded that the Lord Jesus re-stated the principles of Genesis 2:24. Read Matthew 19:4-6 and Mark 10:6-9. He concluded by saying, "... so then they are no more twain, but one flesh. What therefore God hath joined together, let not man put asunder." In other words, He was stressing the *lifelong* character of the relationship. Marriage is not something to be entered into carelessly, and lightly discarded. It should be a solemn commitment—for life—of husband to wife and wife to husband. Paul likewise re-stated Genesis 2:24 in Ephesians 5:31. This repetition surely stresses the importance of the principle stated.

These restrictions should not be regarded as the intent of God to limit our freedom, to restrict our happiness. The God who made us knows best what will bring stability to society and true joy and blessing to His creatures.

When you have mastered this lesson, take the first part of Exam 1 (covering Lesson 1), questions 1-10 on pages 21-22 (right after Lesson 2).

LESSON 1

PERSONAL QUESTIONS TO PONDER

(Write out your answers to these questions. You may, if you wish, submit your answers to your instructor for comment and evaluation.)

1) Does the Bible teach that woman is inferior to man? Do I feel inferior? Why?

_____

_____

_____

_____

2) How can I show acceptance of the headship of man in my life?

_____

_____

_____

_____

	YES	NO
3) Is my marriage what God intended a marriage to be?	___	___
If not,		
are my attitudes partly to blame?	___	___
am I refusing the role of helper and wanting to be leader?	___	___
Face up to your true feelings. Do you chafe at the role God assigned to you as a woman? (Many women do.)	___	___

Pray that God will give you the right attitude of heart, a spirit

11

yielded to Him, and an eagerness to have His good purpose worked out in your life.

MY PERSONAL PRAYER

_____

_____

_____

_____

_____

_____

Sin and its Effects
(Genesis 3)

Before studying Genesis three, read again chapter 2:16, 17. Note how clear God's commandment was: you *may* do this; you *must not* do that! And the warning is given of the penalty for disobedience. Man, as a moral being, was subjected to a test. He could choose to love and obey God, or choose to please himself and disobey God. (How often in the many choices we make in life do we choose as Adam and Eve did!)

We are not told how long the man and the woman lived together in peace and harmony in the beautiful, fruitful garden where God had placed them. But one day the peace was shattered—and the tragedy was brought about by the woman! Was she lingering near the forbidden tree in the midst of the garden? Playing with the thought of what it might give her? If so, she would have been readily vulnerable to the tempter, and he no doubt was alert for any opportunity. We need to stay as far away as possible from temptation, never to dally with that which might lead to sin.

THE TEMPTATION

By his clever questioning and lies, the serpent caused the woman to doubt both God's Word and His love. "Has God withheld something from you? Why? Nothing bad will happen if you eat. God just doesn't want you to be as great as He is. The fruit is delicious—see how beautiful it looks—and it will make you wise!" Such was the serpent's approach, appealing to both appetite and pride.

THE SIN

What was the woman's response? She *considered* the whole proposition! *God* had spoken: what right had she to bring God's Word under her judgment? Eve sinned the moment she believed Satan instead of God. God had said: "Thou shalt surely die." The serpent said: "Ye shall *not* surely die!" She listened to another voice than God's; she coveted something for herself that God had forbidden. Turning from all the bounty that God had given her and from confidence in His love, she took the fruit and ate and then involved her husband too.

It's interesting to note how similar was Satan's approach in his testing of the Lord Jesus in the wilderness (Matthew 4:1-10). Three times he tempted the Lord to take something for Himself that God was not giving Him; three times He refused, quoting and relying on God's Word. *He* held no dialogue with Satan.

Today Satan uses the same tactics in tempting us, dangling before us the glittering things of the world so that we will covet them. The Apostle John warns us about this: "Love not the world, neither the things that are in the world.... the lust of the flesh [Eve saw that the tree was good for food], the lust of the eyes [she saw that it was pleasant to the eyes], and the pride of life [it was desired to make one wise] is not of the Father, but is of the world" (1 John 2: 15, 16). Our strength to resist temptation comes from knowing the Word of God and accepting the will of God.

Eve sinned not only against God, but against Adam as well by acting independently of him. She took the place of leadership that should have been his—and what tragedy resulted! When we violate God's order and step out of our assigned role, we can expect nothing but disorder and grief.

THE RESULTS

The immediate result of sin was shame and guilt, replacing their former state of innocence. The first symptom of sin was in the husband-wife relationship (Genesis 3:7). Sin spoiled the perfect oneness of Genesis 2:23-25.

The serpent had promised that they would know good and evil, and indeed they did. They now knew good, but without the power to do it, and they knew evil, without the power to resist it! And the far-reaching result of sin was death, *as God had said.* There are three phases of death: 1) separation from God, which befell Adam and Eve immediately, 2) physical death, which came years later, and 3) eternal death, eternal separation from God which is the lot of those who refuse God's salvation. Man grasped at exalting himself to be like God (3:5) but doomed himself to death and return to the *dust!*

Notice the contrast we find in Philippians 2:5-11. The Lord Jesus, "existing in the form of God, counted not the being on an equality with God a thing to be grasped, but emptied Himself ... Wherefore God highly exalted Him." "Humble yourselves therefore under the mighty hand of God, that He may exalt you..." (1 Peter 5:6).

The entrance of sin spoiled the happy relationship between man and God. Now the man and the woman were afraid of God and tried to hide from Him. God called them out of hiding, and ever since that day God has been pursuing men in grace, with a view to helping and blessing them in spite of their sin.

THE PENALTY

God dealt with each of the three persons involved in this drama. He cursed the serpent and the ground (Genesis 3:14, 17), but not the man or the woman. He changed the serpent to a lower form of life, symbol of the degradation of Satan who is called "that old serpent" (Revelation 12:9); and He pronounced the ultimate doom of Satan—"her seed ... shall bruise thy head" (Genesis 3:15). The sentence on the man was that the highest activity of his life, *work,* would now be accompanied by toil, travail and weariness, and that eventually his body would return to the dust from which it had been made.

The woman's sentence related primarily to her as wife and mother (3:16). Her distinctive and blessed function, motherhood, was to be associated with pain and sorrow. The Eastern woman's strongest passion has always been the possession of children. She would have her desire, but crossed with sorrow—a reminder that suffering came with sin. Her relationship with her husband was altered: she was now to be subject to his authority, to be ruled by him. In her sin Eve had

15

been the leader and Adam had followed her; now she would be in subjection to him.

Desire for marriage, yet bondage in it, has been the lot of the majority of women since the Fall. Up to that point we find no mention of subordination, though the order of creation implied the leadership of Adam. Now it is stated, "He shall *rule* over thee" (3:16). The history of women, especially in heathen lands, has been a record of subservience and degradation. This is radically altered only when Christianity comes in to change men and society.

The word for "sorrow" in verse 16 and again in verse 17 means toil or travail, so in a sense the sentence on the man and the woman was similar. Labor to the point of weariness, pain, and sorrow were to be their lot.

But note how the grace of God shines on even the darkest situation. Though the woman was first in transgression, she was to have the honor of playing a part in God's plan of redemption. *Her* seed would destroy Satan. The seed of Eve, who had been the serpent's victim, would destroy him (3:15). We see the fulfillment of this promise in Hebrews 2:14—Since men share flesh and blood, Jesus also became a human being (born of a woman) "that through death He might destroy him that had the power of death, that is, the devil."

WOMAN'S PLACE TODAY

In a fallen world full of people governed by sinful human nature it is necessary that authority be established and maintained. This is true alike for the family, the community and the nation. The principle laid down by God that the man should be the head of the family, with authority and responsibility for its well-being, is ultimately for the good of marriage and society. Any woman who wishes to make a success of her marriage will do well to take heed. For the Christian wife there is further instruction in the New Testament. "Wives, submit yourselves unto your own husbands, as unto the Lord. For the husband is the head of the wife, even as Christ is the head of the church" (Ephesians 5:22, 23). This will be discussed in more detail in a future lesson. We merely point out here that this is a continuing principle, that submission is God's will for us, and that He has planned it—for our blessing! How many of us would really choose to shoulder the burden of making decisions and bearing full responsibil-

16

ity for the family? God "knoweth our frame" (Psalm 103:14). He planned for us—and fitted us for—a supportive ministry, not for headship in the family.

Concerning the unmarried woman, nothing is stated in the early chapters of Genesis. Marriage was the norm for women, and still is. Nevertheless, it seems clear from the order and stated purpose of her creation that the role of the woman is supportive and complementary—"a *help* meet for man." Elisabeth Elliot writes: "I do not hold all men to be so strong, so intelligent, so competent, and so virtuous or holy that they deserve a superior position. I simply see that the place is theirs, not by merit, but by appointment."[1]

Do we find the thought of submission hard? Do we question the love of God in ordaining it for us? Then let us pray for God's help in accepting it. The way to a life of peace and rest is through submission to the will of God in every aspect of our lives. The Lord Jesus Himself said, "Not as I will, but as Thou wilt" (Matthew 26:39). The Lord Jesus also said, "Take My yoke upon you and learn of Me, for *I* am meek and lowly in heart—and ye shall find rest unto your souls" (Matthew 11:29).

"Drop thy still dews of quietness
  Till all our strivings cease;
Take from our souls the strain and stress
  And let our ordered lives confess
  The beauty of thy peace."

(J. G. Whittier)

MEMORY VERSE ASSIGNMENT

Memorize Genesis 3:15. This verse shows that God's grace was shown to the woman in His promise of a coming Redeemer.

[1]Elisabeth Elliot Leitch, "A Christian View of Women's Liberation," *Interest*, November, 1975

When you are ready, complete Exam 1 by answering questions 11-20 on pages 23-24. (You should have already answered questions 1-10 as part of your study of Lesson 1.)

LESSON 2

PERSONAL QUESTIONS TO PONDER

(Write out your answers to these questions. You may, if you wish, submit your answers to your instructor for comment and evaluation.)

1) Do I ever choose to please myself even though it means disobeying God? What is the result, even in a small matter? Pleasure—or unrest?

_____

_____

_____

_____

2) How do I handle temptations—enticements to do wrong or to imaginings that are not helpful? Do I think about them, consider and play with them?

_____

_____

_____

_____

3) We saw how Eve brought about tragedy and grief when she stepped outside God's order and took leadership for herself. Do I really believe that disorder and grief will follow if _I_ step out of the role God meant for me as a woman?

_____

_____

_____

_____

Pray for a realization of the enormity of the consequences of sinning and disobeying God. There are no "little" sins. Pray for submission of heart to God's will. "Shall the thing formed say to Him who formed it, Why hast thou made me thus?" (Romans 9:20).

MY PERSONAL PRAYER

_____

_____

_____

_____

_____

_____

_____

_____

_____

THE WOMAN WHO PLEASES GOD

Exam 1
Lessons 1 and 2

Name _____
(print plainly)

Exam
Grade _____

Address_____

City_____ State _____ Zip Code_____ Class Number _____

Instructor _____

LESSON 1

In the blank space in the right-hand margin write the letter of the correct answer. (50 points)

1. The Bible says that the origin of man and his world
   a. was the work of an intelligent Creator
   b. came about by chance
   c. cannot be determined by us
   d. occurred ten million years ago
   _____

2. God rested from His work because
   a. things were not turning out as He wanted
   b. His labor had tired Him
   c. His work was completed and satisfying
   d. He wanted to wait to see what man would do
   _____

3. The key to a happy and fulfilled life is to
   a. stand up for our rights
   b. choose our goals for life and work toward them
   c. function according to God's plan for us
   d. satisfy our physical desires
   _____

4. Genesis 1:27, 28 clearly states that
   a. only man was created in God's image
   b. man alone was given dominion over the earth
   c. man is superior to woman
   d. men and women are equals before God in nature and dominion
   _____

5. The woman was created
   a. from the dust
   b. from Adam
   c. before Adam
   d. to be completely independent of Adam
   _____

21

6. The order of creation of man and woman signifies
   a. that woman is inferior to man
   b. that woman is a higher creation than man
   c. nothing
   d. that man has the responsibility of leadership _____

7. Woman was intended to
   a. cooperate with man and complete him
   b. compete with man
   c. be simply the bearer of children
   d. be man's servant _____

8. The New Testament teaches that
   a. man was created for the woman
   b. man is the head of the woman
   c. a woman may be in a position of authority over man in the church
   d. none of the above is true _____

9. Marriage is
   a. a Christian institution
   b. not part of God's plan for men and women
   c. established by God for our blessing
   d. not an essential basis for human society _____

10. According to God's plan, a marriage should
    a. last only as long as love lasts
    b. be broken up at the request of either partner
    c. not be taken too seriously
    d. be the union of one man and one woman for life _____

WHAT DO YOU SAY?

My fulfillment as a woman lies in ...

_____

_____

_____

_____

_____

22

LESSON 2

In the blank space in the right-hand margin write the letter of the correct answer. (50 points)

11. God's command in Genesis 2:16, 17 was given
    a. so that man wouldn't eat poisonous fruit
    b. so that man wouldn't become as great as God
    c. as a test of man's loyalty and obedience to God
    d. because God didn't really love man

    _____

12. The serpent, in tempting Eve,
    a. quoted God's word exactly
    b. made her question God's love
    c. told her nothing but the truth
    d. was no different from any other creature of the field

    _____

13. The woman responded to the serpent by
    a. rejecting his suggestion immediately
    b. telling him exactly what God had said
    c. considering his suggestion before making a decision
    d. turning away from the tree and the temptation

    _____

14. When Satan tested the Lord Jesus in the wilderness, the Lord
    a. was strongly tempted to take something for Himself that God was not giving Him
    b. carefully considered Satan's suggestions
    c. yielded to Satan as Eve had done
    d. answered by quoting the Word of God

    _____

15. Satan tempts us, as he did Eve, by appealing to
    a. "the lust of the flesh"
    b. "the lust of the eyes"
    c. "the pride of life"
    d. all of the above

    _____

16. Which of the following was **NOT** one of the results of eating the fruit of the tree?
    a. helpful knowledge
    b. shame
    c. fear
    d. death

    _____

17. God's response to sin was to
   a. pronounce a curse on Adam and Eve
   b. forgive Adam and Eve
   c. curse the serpent
   d. blame Eve alone for disobedience _____

18. The woman's penalty
   a. related to her as a wife
   b. didn't alter her relationship with her husband
   c. limited the number of children she could have
   d. didn't affect her in childbearing _____

19. From memory quote Genesis 3:15

   "_____

   _____

   _____

   _____ "

20. Leadership was given to Adam because
   a. he was more intelligent than Eve
   b. he was stronger than Eve
   c. he was holier than Eve
   d. God assigned it to him _____

WHAT DO YOU SAY?

Do you find the idea of submission hard? If so, what are you going to do about it?

_____

_____

_____

_____

_____

Lessons from the Past

For the carrying out of His purposes, God often works through the lives of ordinary men and women, using ordinary human experiences. But in the pages of the Old Testament we find the names of certain women standing out for one reason or another, and we will focus our attention on some of these to see what may be learned from them. Some women worked *with* God; some worked *against* Him; some tried to help God out; some were used by God in spite of themselves.

WOMEN WHO WORKED WITH GOD

Among the devout and spiritual women of the Old Testament is *Jochebed,* the mother of Moses. The simple narrative of Exodus 1:22; 2:1-10 does not tell us in so many words what she was like, but she must have been a woman of *perception* ("she saw that he was a goodly child"), of *courage* ("she hid him three months"—she "was not afraid of the king's commandment"—Hebrews 11:23), of *action* (she made a basket, put the child in it and laid it at the edge of the river, setting his sister to watch), and of *faith* (Hebrews 11:23). But it is in the character of the son that we learn more of the mother. Why was it that Moses, when he came of age, turned his back on the palace and chose "to suffer affliction" with God's people, declaring them to be his people (Hebrews 11:24, 25)? Who taught him about God? About

God's chosen people? About God's promise to deliver them from bondage in Egypt? Can we not see the faithful mother, in the few short years she had him, patiently teaching the little child lessons that were to bear fruit after many days? Moses was one of the greatest characters of history, but the one entrusted with molding his character, the one who gave him his life's vision, was his mother. She worked with God.

Perhaps two centuries later, God needed a man to lead His people. The nation of Israel was in a state of declension and confusion; He wanted a Samuel. So He began with a woman, a woman of faith and prayer (1 Samuel 1:1—2:11).

Hannah was childless. This was a real reproach and calamity in those days, so she sought the Lord's help. She prayed long and earnestly for "a man child" that she might give him to the Lord. The Lord gave her Samuel, and with loving care she prepared him for the role he was to play—for a life different from other boys' lives, as he was separated from home and family and set apart to serve God. What lessons she must have taught him—about the holy God, self-denial and sacrifice, the honor of his calling. And what an example she herself was!

Think of the cost to Hannah of giving up little Samuel, the child she had waited for so long. Who would care for him in the temple? Eli the priest was very aged, and his sons were evil men. How could she leave him in such a place? But Hannah had vowed, and she would perform her vow at whatever cost. As she left Samuel in the temple, she did not weep, but worshipped the Lord in a song (1 Samuel 2:1-11) that is one of the finest specimens we have of Hebrew poetry. It is full of praise to God for His goodness to all humble and earnest hearts.

God still uses human instruments. Are we willing to give up what is most precious to us for His sake? Hannah was glad she did. Her son was both a judge and a prophet—a blessing to his whole nation. And the Lord blessed Hannah in giving her other children (1 Samuel 2:21). Hannah worked with God.

Unlike Jochebed and Hannah, two mothers who were well known because of their sons, *Deborah* held a position of prominence in Israel that was unusual for a woman (Judges 4:4). In her time there was no king in Israel. The nation had forsaken God and followed after

26

heathen gods, so the Lord "sold them into the hands of their enemies" (Judges 2:14). When the people cried to the Lord in distress, He raised up judges to deliver them, only to see them return time and again to their idolatry. In Deborah's time Israel was oppressed by Jabin, king of Canaan, the captain of whose army was Sisera.

We read that Deborah was a prophetess. She had spiritual discernment to hear God's voice and the ability to communicate His Word to others. The people came to her for judgment and counsel (Judges 4:4, 5). Stirred by the pitiable condition of her nation, Deborah called for action. She summoned Barak and gave him the Lord's command to go into battle. When Barak refused to go without her, she agreed to go with him—not to fight, but to give moral support and spiritual help (4:14). The Lord gave victory, and Deborah judged Israel for forty years (5:31).

God did not often place a woman in a position of public prominence, but did not hesitate to do so when the need arose. How blessed for Deborah that she was at hand when God needed her! Jochebed, Hannah and Deborah worked with God, influencing a whole nation, having a part in the ongoing purposes of God. We, too, can be "workers together with God" (1 Corinthians 3:9). Could we ask for anything greater for our lives?

WOMEN WHO WORKED AGAINST GOD

Unhappily, we read of other women who were a blight on their families and their nations—women like Jezebel, queen of Israel, and Athaliah, queen of Judah, who set themselves to do evil and to turn the people from the worship of God to idols. Their wicked influence did much to speed the decline and overthrow of their nations.

Jezebel was a heathen princess and became the wife of Ahab, king of Israel (1 Kings 16:31). She was an idolatress and brought her worship of Baal with her into Israel, causing her husband to "provoke the Lord God of Israel to anger" (1 Kings 16:33). She personally supported 850 prophets of heathen gods (1 Kings 18:19); she slew the prophets of the Lord (1 Kings 18:13); and vowed to kill the prophet Elijah (1 Kings 19:1, 2). Of Ahab it was written: "There was none like unto Ahab, which did sell himself to work wickedness in the sight of the Lord, whom Jezebel his wife stirred up" (1 Kings 21:25, 26).

Athaliah was the daughter of Ahab and Jezebel and she became the wife of Jehoram, king of Judah (2 Kings 8:18). When her husband died, her son Ahaziah came to the throne. Both husband and son "walked in the way of the house of Ahab and did evil in the sight of the Lord" (2 Kings 8:18, 27). At the death of her son, Athaliah "arose and destroyed the seed royal" (2 Kings 11:1) so that she might reign over the land. In the purpose of the Lord, the youngest son escaped, but Athaliah reigned for six years. When the young rightful king was brought forth and crowned and Athaliah was killed, "all the people of the land rejoiced" (2 Kings 11:20).

It is worth noting that often in the book of 2 Kings we are told the names of the mothers of kings. We read, for example, in 2 Kings 21:1, 2—"Manasseh was twelve years old when he began to reign ... And his mother's name was Hephzibah. And he did that which was evil in the sight of the Lord." Likewise in 2 Kings 23:36, 37— "Jehoiakim was twenty and five years old when he began to reign ... And his mother's name was Zebudah ... And he did that which was evil in the sight of the Lord."

We also read of mothers whose sons "did that which was right in the sight of the Lord." (See 2 Kings 12:1, 2; 18:1-3; 22:1, 2). Dare we see a connection between the mention of the king's mother and the description of his character? If the influence of godly mothers like Jochebed and Hannah was reflected in their sons, and the influence of wicked, idol-worshipping queens in their sons, what a responsibility rests on Christian mothers today! We must be aware of the extent and power of our influence—that it is possible in our very homes to work against God.

In what ways can we work against God? We're not idol-worshippers, turning our families away from God! It's true that we don't worship graven images, but twentieth-century Christians have their idols too. What about materialism and success and security? An idol is anything that comes between the soul and God. What goals do we have for ourselves? Bigger and better everything—more comfort and leisure and security through our possessions? What goals do we have for our children? Success in *this* life, for which we carefully prepare them from babyhood, sparing no cost? We need constantly to keep before our children and ourselves the relative importance of time and eternity—

"Only one life; 'twill soon be past,
Only what's done for Christ will last."

WOMEN WHO TRIED TO HELP GOD OUT

Sarah and *Rebekah* were the wives of the patriarchs Abraham and Isaac, and they believed God's word. But they were not content to *wait* for God to act. They tried to bring about what He had promised by schemes of their own.

God had promised Abraham a seed like the stars for number (Genesis 15:5), but his wife Sarah was barren. To hurry things along, to help God out, Sarah suggested a course that might produce an heir (Genesis 16:1, 2). Her scheme worked and Ishmael was born, but he was not the son God had promised. He was a source of irritation in the home, and his descendants have troubled Israel ever since.

God had told Rebekah before her twin sons were born that the elder would serve the younger. The younger son, Jacob, was her favorite, and when she thought this promise of God was about to be defeated, she planned to help God bring His promise to pass. Read about it in Genesis 27:1—28:5. Her scheme worked, in that Jacob received the blessing of the firstborn as God had promised, but she wrecked the peace of her home. She alienated Esau; she never saw Jacob again; and she missed the joy of seeing God work things out in His own way.

Hebrews tells us the need for faith *and* patience (Hebrews 10:36). Why doesn't God answer our prayers right away? Because God's timing isn't always the same as ours, and the waiting strengthens our faith. It's a blessed thing to wait on the Lord and to watch Him work things out for us. He doesn't need our feeble efforts to help; it rejoices His heart to see our faith and our quiet waiting for Him (Psalm 27:14).

WOMEN WHO WERE USED BY GOD IN SPITE OF THEMSELVES

It is encouraging to see how God in His grace uses even those who have failed, in order to accomplish His ends. *Eve,* in spite of her sin, had the assurance that her seed would defeat Satan (Genesis 3:15).

29

Sarah, who had been wrong in the matter of Ishmael, became the mother of the child of promise (Genesis 21:2). *Rahab,* the Gentile harlot, because she believed in God (Joshua 2), became an ancestress of the Messiah (Matthew 1:5). *Naomi,* after the wasted years in Moab, brought her daughter-in-law Ruth under the shelter of the God of Israel and to a position of honor as the wife of Boaz and the great-grandmother of great King David (Ruth 1 and 3:13-17). Queen *Esther,* in spite of her hesitation and fear of the king's anger, had courage to speak to him for her people and was the means of their deliverance (Esther 4:16).

Whatever our character, education, gifts, position in life, God can use us for His glory. The more closely we walk with Him and the more we desire to work with Him, the greater will be our usefulness and our blessing. Remember the old chorus that children sing:

Shamgar had an oxgoad, David had a sling,
Dorcas had a needle, Rahab had some string,
Samson had a jawbone, Aaron had a rod,
Mary had some ointment—but they all were used by God!

FURTHER STUDY

Make your own personal detailed study of all the women mentioned in this lesson.

When you have mastered this lesson, take the first part of Exam 2 (covering Lesson 3), questions 1-10 on pages 41-42 (right after Lesson 4).

LESSON 3

PERSONAL QUESTIONS TO PONDER

(Write out your answers to these questions. You may, if you wish, submit your answers to your instructor for comment and evaluation.)

1) In what ways can I "work with God" today? Has He given me children to "train up" for him? Can I help my husband develop and use his spiritual gifts? Has He given me gifts and opportunities to serve His people? Am I witnessing to an unsaved friend or neighbor? Am I ready, at hand, for God to use me?

_____

_____

_____

_____

2) What kind of influence do I have on my family? Do they see me taken up with the affairs of this life, or keeping the values of eternity in view? What is my desire for my children? In discussing their future (college, advanced training, etc.) have I ever raised the suggestion of missionary work or full-time Christian service at home? If not, why not?

_____

_____

_____

_____

3) Am I ever impatient with God? Do I stop praying for something when God doesn't answer right away? Am I inclined to act on my own initiative rather than wait for God's guidance? How do I

know when to wait and when to act?

_____

_____

_____

_____

4) Do I ever make excuses why God can't use me? Put yourself, as you are, in God's hands and ask Him to use you. He will!

_____

_____

_____

_____

Pray that God will enable you to work with Him in training your children, complementing your husband, influencing your family.

MY PERSONAL PRAYER

_____

_____

_____

_____

_____

_____

_____

A Virtuous Woman
(Proverbs 1-31)

We should not leave our brief study of women in the Old Testament without some consideration of the remarkable woman described in Proverbs 31. But first we notice that in the earlier chapters of the book of Proverbs there are many other references to women, and the majority are far from favorable!

THE STRANGE WOMAN

We read many warnings about "the strange woman" who flatters with her words, forsakes the guide of her youth, forgets the covenant of her God—whose feet go down to death and whose steps take hold on hell (2:16-19; 5:3-8). In chapter 7 we have a detailed account of how "the strange woman" entices "the simple ones," the youths void of understanding. The chapter concludes: "She hath cast down many wounded; yea, many strong men have been slain by her. Her house is the way to hell..." (7:26, 27).

Warning after warning is given. "Keep thee from the evil woman, from the flattery of the tongue of a strange woman. Lust not after her beauty in thy heart ... Can a man take fire in his bosom and his clothes not be burned?... Whoso committeth adultery with a woman lacketh understanding: he that doeth it destroyeth his own soul" (6:24-35).

In chapter 9 she is called "a foolish woman:... she is simple and knoweth nothing," but the conclusion is the same—"her guests are in the depths of hell" (9:13-18).

What a contrast we see between the stern view which God takes of adultery and other sexual sins, and the lightness with which people regard them today! God commanded, through Moses, "Thou shalt not commit adultery" (Exodus 20:14). The Lord Jesus said, "Ye have heard that it was said by them of old time, Thou shalt not commit adultery: But I say unto you, That whosoever looketh on a woman to lust after her hath committed adultery with her in his heart" (Matthew 5:27, 28). Paul wrote, "Flee fornication ... he that committeth fornication sinneth against his own body" (1 Corinthians 6:18). And again, "Be not deceived: neither fornicators ... nor adulterers ... shall inherit the kingdom of God" (1 Corinthians 6:9, 10). The writer to the Hebrews said, "fornicators and adulterers God will judge" (Hebrews 13:4).

The lesson is clear that the woman who wants to please God will shun all impurity of thought and conduct, and will be careful in her words, dress and actions not to cause temptation to any man. We need to be aware that the clothing we wear can be provocative, and that carelessness in the way we sit can arouse others sexually and cause them to sin (Matthew 5:28). Our manner of dress to a great extent reveals what we *are* and what are the intents of our hearts.

Other women are pictured for us in Proverbs. Several times we read of a *contentious* woman, and the writer declares, "It is better to dwell in the wilderness than with a contentious and an *angry* woman" (21:19). "It is better to dwell in a corner of the housetop than with a *brawling* woman in a wide house" (21:9). Again we note a contrast, between this kind of woman and the woman who pleases God. Peter speaks of women who have "the ornament of a meek and quiet spirit, which is in the sight of God of great price" (1 Peter 3:4).

Good women are mentioned also in Proverbs. "A *virtuous* woman is a crown to her husband" (12:4). "Every *wise* woman buildeth her house" (14:1). "Whoso findeth a wife findeth a *good* thing" (18:22). "A *prudent* wife is from the Lord" (19:14). And to sum up, "A *gracious* woman retaineth honor" (11:16). These are qualities we all should covet.

34

THE VIRTUOUS WOMAN

Having taken a wide sweep through Proverbs, we come in the last chapter to the description of a truly remarkable woman. The chapter opens: "The words of King Lemuel, the prophecy that his mother taught him." (Read all of Proverbs 31.) Was his mother describing the kind of woman he should look for in a wife? Or was Lemuel describing the kind of woman his mother was? We cannot tell, but we remark in passing that each man gets his ideal of womanhood from someone who has influenced his life. Are we always aware of the power of our influence? A mother's influence cannot be overestimated, but what of a sister's? Some of the world's famous men, and some well-known in the church, have been blessed greatly through the love and friendship (and prayers) of a devoted sister. Teachers, too, have a powerful influence. A godly and praying woman in any sphere of life is a power for God, often in ways she does not dream of.

"Who can find a virtuous [morally excellent] woman?" (31:10). "Her price is far above rubies." In the Orient a bride was actually purchased, and even today in some lands a "bride price" is demanded by the girl's father. This virtuous woman would bring a high price indeed—"far above rubies"—a rare fortune.

"The heart of her husband doth safely trust in her" (v. 11). This first statement sums up all that follows. In relation to her husband, family, household, and the outside world, she is completely trustworthy; her husband's heart can be at rest. In the Hebrew home the mother was the presiding genius. A man attached great importance to the welfare and reputation of his family, to material prosperity and good standing in the community. The wife and mother bore the responsibility of achieving many of these desirable objectives. Because of her diligence and faithfulness, her husband was free to concentrate on his calling and to sit "in the gates ... among the elders of the land" (v. 23)—a position of honor and respect in the city council. "She will do him good and not evil all the days of her life" (v. 12). Here is a good resolution for every bride.

In relation to her household affairs this woman is diligent (v. 13), enterprising (v. 14), disciplined and well-organized (v. 15), skillful (v. 19), prepared for the future (v. 21), clothed with beauty and dignity (v. 22). She is not afraid of hard work, not lazy, not careless nor slipshod (v. 27). The wheels of her household run smoothly at all times. There is order and peace and well-being in such a home. Surely this is pleasing to God who "is not the author of confusion but of peace" (1 Corinthians 14:33), and who says in connection with His house, "Let all things be done decently and in order" (1 Corinthians 14:40).

Far from being overwhelmed by running a large household, this woman has time and energy for conducting business outside her home. She buys a field and plants a vineyard (v. 16). She makes fine linen and weaves girdles, then sells them to the merchants (v. 24). "She perceives that her merchandise is good" (v. 18). Her work is of good quality; she would not stoop to make and sell anything shoddy. This principle should characterize us also. "Whatsoever ye do, do all to the glory of God" (1 Corinthians 10:31). Only the very finest we are capable of doing will bring honor to our Lord.

What other qualities make up the character of this virtuous woman? She is sympathetic and concerned about the poor and needy (v. 20). Wisdom and kindness characterize her (v. 26). Here is no super-efficient person who rides rough-shod over those around her in order to accomplish her purposes. Kindness is a law of her being. And what a difference a little kindness would make in many of our homes today!

No wonder she was beloved by her husband and children (v. 28)—beloved, not primarily because she was a capable homemaker who cared for the comfort and well-being of her family, nor because she was an able and successful businesswoman, but because she was a wise, kind, sympathetic, loving person (such as we all may be). Most women who read this description in Proverbs 31:10-31 do so with a distinct sense of inferiority! Who could measure up to the accomplishments recorded here? But surely the love and esteem of her family gave her the greatest joy and satisfaction of her life, and this is something each of us may achieve. We need not try to equal her accomplishments: we *should* try to emulate her character—to be trustworthy, diligent, self-disciplined, hard-working, sympathetic, kind, loving.

And one other thing—she was "a woman that feareth the Lord" (v. 30)! Is this the explanation of all that has been said of this woman? Here is her motivation, and here, too, is ours. "The fear of the Lord is the beginning of wisdom" (Proverbs 9:10). There is no way that we can live a life, or develop a character, pleasing to God without beginning with Him. Our own efforts and strivings, turning over new leaves, setting goals for ourselves and the like, may bring a measure of success. But the woman who, in the fear of God, yields herself wholly to the Lord, putting herself into His hands to mold and to use, is the truly blessed woman, whose "works praise her in the gates" (v. 31) and whose family rises up and calls blessed. Her price is far above rubies.

FURTHER STUDY

Read through the book of Proverbs and make a note of all the references to women and categorize these in a way that will prove helpful to you.

When you are ready, complete Exam 2 by answering questions 11-20 on pages 43-44. (You should have already answered questions 1-10 as part of your study of Lesson 3.)

LESSON 4

PERSONAL QUESTIONS TO PONDER

(Write out your answers to these questions. You may, if you wish, submit your answers to your instructor for comment and evaluation.)

1) When I select my clothing, is my aim to draw attention to myself? If current styles are immodest and revealing, do I conform, saying, "Everyone else wears them"? Or do I stop to consider what would be pleasing to the Lord?

_____

_____

_____

_____

2) Can my husband "safely trust in" me—in my discretion (able to keep confidences and not talk everywhere about personal and family affairs), my faithfulness in fulfilling responsibilities, my upholding the honor of his name in every way possible?

_____

_____

_____

_____

3) Does kindness characterize me in my relations with others? Even with my family?

_____

_____

_____

_____

4) Am I trying to produce spiritual growth in my life by my own efforts? To build a character pleasing to God? Or have I put myself into the Lord's hands that *He* may mold me and make me a woman who pleases Him?

_____

_____

_____

_____

Pray that God will give you wisdom in selecting your clothes, in running your home, in developing relationships with others, including your family, in building a character pleasing to God.

MY PERSONAL PRAYER

_____

_____

_____

_____

_____

_____

THE WOMAN WHO PLEASES GOD

Exam 2
Lessons 3 and 4

Name _____
(print plainly)

Exam
Grade _____

Address _____

City _____ State _____ Zip Code _____ Class Number _____

Instructor _____

LESSON 3

In the blank space in the right-hand margin write the letter of the correct answer. (50 points)

1. Jochebed, the mother of Moses,
   a. was afraid of the king of Egypt
   b. despaired of saving her child from death
   c. had to give up her son before he was old enough to teach him about God
   d. taught him about God and His promise to deliver His people _____

2. Hannah, the mother of Samuel,
   a. knew that the temple was a good place for a child to grow up
   b. wept when she left him in the temple
   c. kept her vow at great cost to herself
   d. complained that the Lord had taken her son from her _____

3. Deborah, the prophetess,
   a. was one of many women judges in Israel
   b. told the people not to fight against Sisera
   c. refused to go to the battle with Barak
   d. judged Israel for forty years _____

4. Jezebel, queen of Israel,
   a. helped her husband and nation
   b. stirred up Ahab to do evil
   c. was a worshipper of Jehovah
   d. supported the prophets of the Lord _____

5. Athaliah, queen of Judah,
   a. was the sister of Jezebel
   b. helped her husband and son to do what was right
   c. destroyed the royal family so she could be ruler of the land
   d. was mourned by the people when she died _____

6. In the book of 2 Kings,
   a. the names of the mothers of kings are frequently mentioned
   b. it is said that the mothers of the kings always influenced them for good
   c. there seems to be no connection between the mothers and the characters of their sons
   d. all the kings did "evil in the sight of the Lord" _____

7. In our day,
   a. materialism and success are idols to many Christians
   b. a Christian mother can't work against God
   c. we don't have any idols
   d. most Christians stress the importance of eternity over this life _____

8. Sarah, the wife of Abraham,
   a. didn't believe God's word
   b. believed God but couldn't wait for Him to act
   c. waited patiently for the son God had promised
   d. did God's will in the birth of Ishmael _____

9. The story of Rebekah shows us
   a. that scheming to help God out is a good idea
   b. that God sometimes needs our help or His promises will fail
   c. how to have a happy home life
   d. that we need faith and patience in order to please God _____

10. In order to accomplish His ends, God uses
   a. only those who have never failed
   b. only those who are educated and gifted
   c. only those who are young and free from responsibility
   d. each one who is yielded to Him and desires His glory _____

WHAT DO YOU SAY?

Is there an idol in your life—anything that comes between you and God?

_____

_____

_____

_____

LESSON 4

In the blank space in the right-hand margin write the letter of the correct answer. (50 points)

11. The "strange woman" of Proverbs was said to be
a. wise
b. happy
c. foolish and evil
d. on her way to heaven   _____

12. In God's view, fornication and adultery
a. are not serious sins
b. are all right between consenting adults
c. are not harmful as long as no one is hurt
d. call for stern judgment   _____

13. Proverbs mentions two contrasting kinds of women. Fill in the blanks in the following descriptions:
1. A woman who is contentious, _____ and _____.

2. A woman who is wise, _____ and _____.

14. Proverbs chapter 31 was written by
a. King Solomon
b. King Lemuel
c. Lemuel's mother
d. King David   _____

15. The "bride price" is
a. money paid to the girl's father by the groom
b. money paid by the girl's father to the husband
c. money the girl saves for her marriage
d. an old custom not carried on today   _____

16. The heart of a husband is restful if his wife is
   a. rich
   b. talented
   c. trustworthy
   d. beautiful   _____

17. A well-ordered household
   a. requires little effort
   b. needs little planning and organization
   c. is really not important
   d. brings peace and well-being to the family   _____

18. From the example of the "virtuous woman" we see that
   a. women have no business ability
   b. trying to do business outside the home doesn't work
   c. a capable, disciplined woman can run both a home and a business without neglecting her family responsibilities
   d. all women should hold outside jobs.   _____

19. Which of the following is **NOT** said of the virtuous woman?
   a. She stretches out her hand to the poor and needy
   b. She grows and prepares all her own food
   c. She speaks with wisdom
   d. Kindness characterizes all she says   _____

20. The secret of this woman's life was that
   a. she was motivated by fear and reverence for the Lord
   b. she had unusual strength and ability
   c. she had many servants to help her
   d. she was a good self-starter   _____

WHAT DO YOU SAY?

How well do you measure up to the character of the virtuous woman?

_____

_____

_____

_____

_____

The Lord Jesus and Women

At the time Christ was born, women were held to be inferior creatures by Greeks, Romans and Jews. In *Greece* a woman was under the control and authority of her husband, on the level of a slave. In *Rome* the wife was legally the property of her husband. She had more freedom than the women in Greece, but this led to moral looseness and the increase of divorce. Among the *Jews,* though the woman was considered to be inferior to her husband, she held a place of dignity within her home. But she had few legal rights and no education, even of a religious sort. It was a thoroughly male-dominated society in which Jesus lived.

Against this background, the attitude of Jesus toward women was most remarkable. He showed no prejudice, uttered no derogatory word about women. He appreciated their distinct capabilities and treated them with courtesy and respect.

He had *compassion* for them in their needs. He healed Peter's wife's mother of a fever (Matthew 8:14), the woman with a hemorrhage who touched His garment (Matthew 9:20), the poor woman who had been bent double for eighteen years (Luke 13:11). At Nain He raised the widow's son from death and presented him alive to his mother (Luke 7:12-15). When the woman taken in adultery was brought to Him, He treated her with delicacy and grace (John 8:3).

His words, "Come unto Me ... and I will give you rest," must have had great appeal to the women, who bore such heavy burdens, and who were drawn to Him by His sympathy. Even from the Cross He showed compassion in the thought He had for His mother (John 19:25-27).

He spoke words of *commendation* to some women. To the Syrophenician woman who came to Him asking that her demon-possessed daughter might be delivered, He said, "O woman, great is thy faith" (Matthew 15:21-28). One day, as He sat by the treasury in the temple, He saw rich men putting in their gifts and then watched a poor widow throwing in two mites. He commended her sacrificial giving, saying, "This poor widow hath cast in *more* than they all" (Luke 21:1-4). He noted, not the size of the gift, but the heart of the giver. The rich gave what they would never miss: she gave all that she had and satisfied the heart of God.

He *respected* their intellectual and spiritual capacities. Though no education was given to girls or women, He taught them privately and (in the crowd) publicly. Some of His most profound revelations about Himself and about His Father were given personally to individual women.

In John, chapter four, we read of His encounter at a well with a woman of Samaria. Though the "Jews had no dealings with Samaritans" (4:9), and a Jewish teacher would not speak to a woman in public (not even his wife), the Lord Jesus conversed with this woman who was a social outcast. He spoke to her about worship and the need to worship God in spirit and in truth, since God is a Spirit (4:24). He revealed Himself as the Messiah for whom both Jews and Samaritans looked—a thrilling revelation He had given to no one else! The woman believed and so witnessed about Him in her city that many of her neighbors came to Him and believed also.

At the home of Martha and Mary in Bethany, Mary "sat at Jesus' feet and heard His word" (Luke 10:39). The Lord Jesus made it plain that this was pleasing to Him. He did not relegate Mary to the kitchen but respected her desire and her ability to learn of His teaching. At the same time He did not downgrade Martha's service, but gently showed her that service alone is not enough. We *must* take time to sit at His feet and learn from Him: He wants us more than

He wants our service. What we *are* is more important than what we *do*.

Some time later, Lazarus, the brother of Mary and Martha, fell ill and died. And it was to Martha that the Lord Jesus spoke those thrilling words that have comforted His people ever since: "I am the resurrection and the life: he that believeth in Me, though he were dead, yet shall he live..." (John 11:25).

The Lord Jesus *accepted* the ministry of women. We have just mentioned the home in Bethany where He was welcomed and cared for by the two devoted sisters. We also read of "many women which followed Jesus from Galilee, ministering unto Him" (Matthew 27:55), and of "certain women which ministered to Him of their substance" (Luke 8:2, 3). Apparently there was a group of women who were prepared to suffer the discomforts of an itinerant ministry in order to care for the physical needs of the Lord and His disciples. C. C. Ryrie notes that whenever ministry is spoken of as being rendered directly to Jesus, it is the ministry of either angels or women![1] How blessed to be among those who minister to Him!

The Lord Jesus *appreciated* the affection and gratitude of women. In Luke 7:36-50 we read of an incident that took place in the house of a Pharisee who had invited Jesus to have a meal with him. As the meal progressed, a poor woman "which was a sinner" crept in and stood at His feet weeping. As the tears fell on His feet, she wiped them away with her hair, kissed His feet, and anointed them with costly, sweet-smelling ointment. The Pharisee would have thrust her away without letting her touch him, but Jesus accepted her loving tribute. He said it was because her many sins had been forgiven that she cared so greatly. We should remark in passing that Jesus noticed the Pharisee's neglect as well as appreciating the woman's gratitude (7:44-46). What does He receive from us?

Near the end of the Lord's earthly ministry, a similar incident occurred (John 12:1-8; Matthew 26:6-13). This time He was in the house of His dearly-loved friends in Bethany, and Mary, who had sat at His feet, now brought precious ointment and anointed His feet. As she broke the costly container and poured out its contents, one of the disciples protested at "this waste." But to Mary nothing was too good or too costly to lavish on Him. The Lord commended her, saying she had done a good thing. (Is anything too precious or costly to be expended on *Him?*) How much her devotion must have meant to Him, especially in light of the apparent slowness of the disciples to accept His approaching death. Mary anointed His body in anticipation of His death; the other women who cared for Him were too late, coming with their spices when they were no longer needed (Luke 23:55—24:3). Let us *today* bring to Him the love and worship of redeemed hearts, the "sacrifice of praise ... giving thanks to His Name" (Hebrews 13:15).

The Lord Jesus *honored* women highly by appearing first to them after His resurrection. He gave to women the privilege of carrying the good news of His resurrection to His disciples (Matthew 28:1-10; Mark 16:1-10; Luke 24:1-10; John 20:1-18). As far as we know, none of the disciples was at the cross except John—but the women were there (Matthew 27:55)! And "very early in the morning" of the resurrection day, "when it was yet dark," the women came to the tomb. It was not that their faith was greater than that of the disciples, for they all seemed to have been plunged into despair. Surely it was their love that drew them to where He was—love for this Man who was like no other man and who had transformed their lives. And their love was rewarded—oh, how it was rewarded! Their sorrow was turned into joy, their mourning to singing, when they saw the Lord, risen from the dead, triumphant! And they ran to tell others the glad news.

Love *seeking* Him will ever be rewarded by *seeing* Him. Not to the proud, the mighty, the intellectual does He reveal Himself, but to the humble, loving heart that longs after Him. And the greater the love, the clearer the vision. To Mary's heart cry, "Where is He?" the Lord Himself answered, "Mary." And she saw the One she was seeking. For what are we longing and seeking today? The Lord Jesus said, "He that loveth Me shall be loved of my Father, and I will love him, and *will manifest myself to him*" (John 14:21).

FURTHER STUDY

Study in further detail the Bible passages referred to in this lesson and note for yourself the attitude of the Lord Jesus toward women in each instance.

[1]Charles Caldwell Ryrie, *The Place of Women in the Church* (The Macmillan Company, New York), page 34.

When you have mastered this lesson, take the first part of Exam 3 (covering Lesson 5), questions 1-10 on pages 61-62 (right after Lesson 6).

LESSON 5

PERSONAL QUESTIONS TO PONDER

(Write out your answers to these questions. You may, if you wish, submit your answers to your instructor for comment and evaluation.)

1) From what we've learned of the Lord Jesus' attitude toward women, what do I think is His attitude toward me? Would I be of little account—or important and valuable to Him? Would I feel free to go to Him in need? Would I want to gain His commendation?

_____

_____

_____

_____

2) Is He important to me—so that I want to listen to what He says, like Mary? Am I taking time each day to read His Word and let Him speak to me?

_____

_____

_____

_____

3) For what am I seeking in life? What occupies my thoughts?

_____

_____

_____

Pray that you will discover the Lord Jesus' attitude toward you, that you will gain His commendation, that you will take time each day to sit at His feet, that your thoughts will be filled with Christ.

MY PERSONAL PRAYER

_____

_____

_____

_____

_____

_____

_____

A Composite Picture

Continuing our search for the woman who pleases God, we turn for a look at the characteristics of some of the women named in the New Testament. Very little is told us of any one person: for the most part we get glimpses only. And it is not likely that any one woman could personify God's ideal. For this reason we will make a composite picture, finding in various women traits that are pleasing to God.

SUBMISSION AND OBEDIENCE

We cannot make a better start than with *Mary,* the mother of our Lord. What was it about this young woman that caused her to be favored by God in such a singular way? We are told only that she was a virgin, espoused to Joseph. Surely there must have been purity of life and devotion of heart to God, though we are not told so. Our glimpse into her character comes in her reply to the angel, "Behold the handmaid of the Lord; be it unto me according to thy word" (Luke 1:38). Here was a submissive spirit and a readiness to do God's will. Mary was totally available to God because she trusted in Him. Could anything be more pleasing to God?

Mary appears a number of times in Scripture; we will look at only one more. On the occasion of a wedding in Cana of Galilee (John 2:1-11), Mary gave some advice that cannot be surpassed. She said to the servants, "Whatsoever He saith unto you, do it." We make no mistake when we obey the word of the Lord and submit ourselves wholly to Him.

It should be noted that, though Mary was most blessed and favored by God, she was still in need of salvation like all other men and women. She herself said, "My spirit has rejoiced in God *my Savior*" (Luke 1:47).

RIGHTEOUS AND BLAMELESS

Elisabeth, the mother of John the Baptist and a relative of Mary's, was an older woman—most of her life was past. What was the record of that life? She and her husband, Zacharias, "were both righteous before God, walking in all the commandments and ordinances of the Lord blameless" (Luke 1:6). This is God's desire for all of us, women and men alike: "He hath chosen us ... that we should be holy and without blame before Him" (Ephesians 1:4).

DEVOTION TO GOD

Anna was an aged woman in Jerusalem who "departed not from the temple, but served God with fastings and prayers night and day" (Luke 2:37). She was in the temple when the infant Jesus was brought in to be presented to the Lord, and seeing Him, she gave thanks to God. She saw in Him the redemption of Israel and joyfully spoke of Him to others. Anna's whole life was devoted to God—her time, her energy, all that she had. And we are exhorted to present our "bodies a living sacrifice ... unto God" (Romans 12:1). We are to "seek first the kingdom of God" (Matthew 6:33)—to set our "affection on things above" (Colossians 3:2). On what are our hearts set? To whom are we devoted—self, the world, or God?

LOVE AND GRATITUDE

The name of *Mary Magdalene* is familiar to all as one out of whom Jesus cast seven demons. She is first mentioned in association with other "women which had been healed of evil spirits and infirmities ... which ministered unto Him of their substance" (Luke 8:2, 3). Her love and gratitude for deliverance were so great that she wanted to be with the Lord Jesus to minister to Him, without thought of cost to herself. We see her again, watching, grief-stricken, at the cross

(Matthew 27:55, 56), and then weeping at the tomb (John 20:1-18). There her loving heart was satisfied by the sight of the risen Lord. Mark tells us that He appeared *first* to Mary Magdalene (Mark 16:9). How He rewarded her love and gratitude!

On another occasion the Lord showed that He appreciated gratitude. When He had healed ten lepers and only one came to thank and worship Him, He inquired, "Where are the nine?" (Luke 17:17). Certainly a grateful heart should characterize those who call Jesus Lord.

FAITH

Writing to Timothy, Paul said, "I call to remembrance the unfeigned faith that is in thee, which dwelt first in thy grandmother *Lois* and thy mother *Eunice*" (2 Timothy 1:5). These two women were known for their true faith in God—a faith that was operative in their lives and which they sought to communicate to others. Apparently they carefully taught young Timothy "the holy scriptures" (2 Timothy 3:15) with a view to his salvation. Oh, that such faithfulness and faith in God were found in all mothers and grandmothers, and in all others who have contacts with children!

WORSHIP

Each time we see *Mary of Bethany,* she is at the feet of the Lord Jesus. In Luke 10:38-42 she is sitting at His feet, listening to His words, learning of Him. In John 11:32 she falls at His feet, weeping, in her distress over the death of her brother. In John 12:3 she anoints His feet with costly perfume and wipes them with her hair. And as the fragrance of the perfume filled the house, so the fragrance of her worship rejoiced the heart of the Lord. She was a true worshipper— and the Lord "seeketh such to worship Him" (John 4:23). Someone has defined worship as the overflow of a heart filled with Christ. "O come let us worship and bow down: let us kneel before the Lord our Maker" (Psalm 95:6).

GOOD WORKS

Martha of Bethany seems to be very different from her sister, Mary, and has often been put down as unspiritual—the busy housewife with little time for spiritual things. But "Jesus loved Martha" (John 11:5), and she had a true and loyal faith in Him (John 11:21-27). The Lord appreciates and needs both Marthas and Marys. Martha's problem was that she was "cumbered about *much* serving" (Luke 10:40), and it is all too easy for us, too, to get things out of balance. God values our service for Him, but not at the expense of ourselves. What we are far outweighs in His estimation what we do. We need a proper balance of sitting (at His feet) and serving.

In Acts 9:36-41 we read about *Dorcas,* who was a "disciple ... full of good works and almsdeeds which she did." A complete record of her good works is not given to us, but we know she made coats and garments, and her kindness to widows was such that they wept and mourned at her death. She is called a "disciple," and she proved the reality of the new life within her by her love and care for others. She exemplified the kind of faith James wrote about (James 2:14-26)—a faith that works.

While we are not *saved* by works, we are saved *unto* good works: "God hath before ordained that we should walk in them" (Ephesians 2:9, 10). "To do good and to communicate, forget not" (Hebrews 13:16).

HOSPITALITY

In the city of Philippi lived a "woman named *Lydia,* a seller of purple ... of Thyatira, who worshipped God" (Acts 16:14). She was a Gentile, but she met regularly for prayer with Jewish women and other God-fearing Gentile women like herself. Since there was no synagogue in Philippi, Paul and his company joined this group of women and began to teach them, and "the Lord opened" Lydia's heart. The opened heart led to an opened home, as she "constrained" the missionaries to accept her hospitality. So it was in her home that the first church in Europe began to meet. An opened heart—an opened home—an opened continent!

Peter exhorts us to "use hospitality one to another without grudging" (1 Peter 4:9), and we are further urged "to entertain strangers: for thereby some have entertained angels unawares" (Hebrews 13:2). How many of us may have missed out on the angels because of our lack of hospitality?

SERVICE IN THE GOSPEL

A number of women were named by Paul in Romans 16 as helpers and fellow-workers. *Phoebe* was "a servant of the church at Cenchrea ... a succourer of many." *Priscilla,* Paul's "helper in Christ Jesus," served with her husband in Corinth, Ephesus and Rome. They were "apt to teach," the church met in their house, and they were ready to give their lives for Paul's sake. *Mary* "bestowed much labor on us." *Tryphena* and *Tryphosa* "labored in the Lord." *Persis* "labored much in the Lord." Writing to Philippi, Paul mentions *Euodias* and *Syntyche,* "women which labored with me in the gospel" (Philippians 4:2, 3).

The kind of work these women did is not specified. The words "servant, succourer, helper," would suggest a supportive ministry. There seems to be no scriptural ground for the assumption that these women were engaged in a preaching and teaching ministry like Paul's—as some like to think. That they "labored" and "labored much" shows the zeal and devotion with which they served the Lord. Whatever they did was done heartily as to the Lord, and "with such sacrifices God is well pleased" (Hebrews 13:16).

FURTHER STUDY

Look up the references to other women in the Bible and make a note of their characteristics that you consider would be pleasing to God.

When you are ready, complete Exam 3 by answering questions 11-20 on pages 63-64. (You should have already answered questions 1-10 as part of your study of Lesson 5.)

LESSON 6

PERSONAL QUESTIONS TO PONDER

(Write out your answers to these questions. You may, if you wish, submit your answers to your instructor for comment and evaluation.)

1) Are any of these characteristics, so pleasing to God, true of me?

_____

_____

_____

_____

2) Is there one area—or more than one—where I particularly come short?

_____

_____

_____

_____

3) Will I set myself, with God's help, to follow the example of these women? What goals should I set for myself right now? Begin at once!

_____

_____

_____

_____

Pray that God will help you develop the characteristics He wants in your life, that He will give you grace to address yourself to those areas where you particularly come short, that He will grant you the determination to follow the example of the women referred to in the lesson, that He will guide you in the setting of personal goals, that He will help you begin at once.

MY PERSONAL PRAYER

_____

_____

_____

_____

_____

THE WOMAN WHO PLEASES GOD

Name _____ Exam Grade _____
(print plainly)

Address_____

City_____ State _____ Zip Code_____ Class Number _____

Instructor _____

LESSON 5

In the blank space in the right-hand margin write the letter of the correct answer. (50 points)

1. Which of the following statements is true? At the time of Christ,
   a. in Greece a woman was on the same level as her husband
   b. in Rome women were treated like slaves
   c. among the Jews women were considered to be inferior creatures
   d. men and women everywhere were social equals   _____

2. The Lord Jesus
   a. was prejudiced against women
   b. treated women with respect
   c. rebuked some women publicly
   d. taught that women couldn't be educated   _____

3. The Lord commended the Syrophenician woman for
   a. her faith
   b. her generosity
   c. her love
   d. her intelligence   _____

4. The Lord gave spiritual teaching individually to
   a. Martha
   b. Mary
   c. the woman at the well in Samaria
   d. all of the above   _____

5. In the home of Martha and Mary, the Lord Jesus
   a. commended Martha's service
   b. rebuked Mary's idleness

  c. said that a woman's place is in the kitchen
  d. showed the importance of sitting at His feet   _____

6. The ministry of women
  a. was accepted by the Lord Jesus
  b. was unacceptable to the Lord
  c. was given to the Lord only in Jerusalem
  d. was given by only a few   _____

7. In the incident in the house of the Pharisee in Luke 7,
  a. the Lord wouldn't let the woman touch Him
  b. the Pharisee commended the woman
  c. the Lord appreciated the woman's gratitude
  d. the Lord didn't notice the Pharisee's neglect of courtesy _____

8. When Mary anointed the Lord in Bethany,
  a. He said it was a waste of money
  b. He said it was a good thing
  c. the disciples were pleased
  d. the disciples understood that it was for His burial _____

9. After His resurrection, the Lord Jesus appeared first
  a. to His disciples
  b. to His mother
  c. to some women
  d. to Peter   _____

10. The women were drawn to the tomb by
  a. their faith
  b. their love
  c. their curiosity
  d. their obedience   _____

WHAT DO YOU SAY?

Mary thought that nothing was too costly to lavish on the Lord; what is your attitude?

_____

_____

_____

_____

LESSON 6

In the blank space in the right-hand margin write the letter of the correct answer. (50 points)

11. The Bible shows that Mary, the mother of our Lord,
    a. was pure and righteous
    b. made herself totally available to God
    c. came of a wealthy Jewish family
    d. was sinless and not subject to death _____

12. Elisabeth, the mother of John Baptist,
    a. was a young woman like her cousin Mary
    b. was commended for her good works
    c. carefully kept all the laws and ordinances of God
    d. was dumb until her son was born _____

13. Following Anna's example, we are exhorted to
    a. present ourselves to God
    b. seek first the kingdom of God
    c. set our affection on things above
    d. do all of these things _____

14. Mary Magdalene
    a. ministered to the Lord out of love and gratitude
    b. was an outcast and not allowed to approach the Lord
    c. was afraid to stand by the cross
    d. never saw the Lord after He was crucified _____

15. Eunice, the mother of Timothy,
    a. was a Greek
    b. was the only Christian in her family
    c. was known for her faith
    d. didn't know the Scriptures _____

16. Which of the following is **NOT** told us of Mary of Bethany? We see her
    a. learning at Jesus' feet
    b. weeping at Jesus' feet
    c. kissing Jesus' feet
    d. anointing Jesus' feet _____

63

17. In connection with Martha, we find that the Lord Jesus
     a. preferred to see women stay in the kitchen
     b. loved her more than Mary
     c. found no real faith in her
     d. cares more about what we *are* than what we do _____

18. Lydia, of the city of Philippi,
     a. was a Jewess
     b. was a worshipper of God
     c. did not respond to the gospel Paul preached
     d. refused to give hospitality to Paul and his friends _____

19. Which of the following women was called "a servant of the church"?
     a. Phoebe
     b. Priscilla
     c. Mary
     d. Persis _____

20. In the New Testament, women
     a. engaged in preaching as Paul did
     b. contributed very little to the expansion of Christianity
     c. had a valuable supportive ministry in the spread of the gospel
     d. are not mentioned as helpers by Paul _____

WHAT DO YOU SAY?

Which of the traits described in this lesson as pleasing to God do you need to develop? Will you set yourself to do so?

_____

_____

_____

_____

_____

Women's Role in the Church
(1 Corinthians 11:3-16)

Much has been said and written over the years about the role of women in the church, and it will not be possible to go into much detail here. For those who are interested in pursuing the subject further, the bibliography at the end of the course should be consulted.

From a study of the Scriptures three basic truths are evident: 1) Women and men are equal as far as position before God and spiritual privilege are concerned. 2) Equality of status does not involve identity of function and responsibility. Sexual differences remain. 3) The ministry of women is of great importance for the well-being of the church.

EQUAL—

The apostle Paul, in spite of all the anti-feminist charges against him, exhibited the same attitude toward women as his Lord. He appreciated and joined the women's prayer group at Philippi (Acts 16:13), accepted Lydia's hospitality and planted the first church in Europe in her home. He mentioned Euodias and Syntyche as co-laborers with him (Philippians 4:3, 4) and warmly commended Priscilla and Phoebe and other women for their "much labor" and help in the work of the Lord (Romans 16). He stated very clearly the spiritual equality of men and women. "Ye are all the children of God by faith in Christ Jesus ... There is neither Jew nor Greek ... bond nor free ... male nor female: for ye are all one in Christ Jesus" (Galatians 3:26-28). Male and female, we have the same standing before God. Justified by faith, we have peace with God, enjoy His gracious favor, rejoice in hope of the glory of God (Romans 5:1, 2). But though equality is stated, the differences are not negated. The Jews remained Jews and the Greeks were still Greeks, maleness and femaleness were not altered.

BUT DIFFERENT!

The sexual differences were put there by God at creation and put there for His good purpose. God had different functions and responsibilities in mind for the man and for the woman. *Both* are important for the carrying out of His purposes. God in His sovereignty assigned each of His creatures to its position in the universe. He assigned man to a place of special responsibility and gave to woman a role complementary to man (Genesis 2:18). Superiority and inferiority were not involved: this was simply God's order and plan— equality of status, but difference in function.

We have noticed the Lord Jesus' acceptance and appreciation of women, yet there were no women chosen among the twelve disciples, no women present at the institution of the Lord's Supper, no women missionaries or writers of the New Testament, no women leaders of the churches. It seems obvious that the place of leadership, of public prominence, was not meant for women, but that is not to say that the role of women is insignificant and of little value.

WOMEN'S MINISTRY

All believers, women as well as men, have received spiritual gifts for ministry in the body of Christ. All are important to the well-being of the local church. It is only as *everyone* ministers that the needs of the whole body are met (Ephesians 4:16). If we have no ministry in the church, it is not for lack of gift or opportunity, but because of our own inner barrenness. We will be discussing spiritual gifts and their use in Lesson 12.

We have seen in Lesson 6 something of the ministry of women in the New Testament—the praise and worship, hospitality, teaching, good works, labor in the gospel—for which they were noted. Women were in the upper room prayer meeting with the disciples after the Lord's ascension (Acts 1:14). They were probably present in Acts 2 at the descent of the Spirit. Many women were saved in the early days of the church (Acts 5:14). They were subjected to persecution just as the men were (Acts 8:3). They made valuable contributions to the expansion of Christianity in the first century. Gary Inrig says, "There is no gift which God has given to a woman that the church does not need and that cannot be actively and creatively used in a biblical way to glorify the Lord Jesus."[1]

What does he mean by "used in a biblical way"? We must determine from the whole tenor and teaching of the New Testament just *how* God wants us to serve Him. The soldier may be highly trained and fully equipped, but he doesn't act on his own initiative; he waits for the direction of his commander. Someone has said, "For best results, obey instructions of maker!" We want to know the instructions of the Head of the church, as He has revealed them to us in His Word. It is not God's purpose to *suppress* the gifts He has given to women, but to lay out the framework in which they are to be used.

HEADSHIP AND SUBMISSION

The principles of headship, submission and authority are evident throughout the Bible, beginning with the order of creation. Adam was formed first, then Eve. The one formed first is to have the responsibility of authority; the one formed after is to follow and be in subjection. "The man is not of the woman, but the woman of the man. Neither was the man created for the woman, but the woman for the man" (1 Corinthians 11:8, 9). Women react defensively to the order of creation, because men have wrongly assumed that priority means superiority and have acted in a domineering way. This was not God's intention.

The Apostle Paul states the principle of headship very clearly: "... the head of every man is Christ; and the head of the woman is the man; and the head of Christ is God" (1 Corinthians 11:3). Thus there are three great relationships involving subordination. Such headship

67

is not intended to downgrade anyone. Was Christ inferior because He was subordinate? The headship of God in relation to Christ was no threat to His Person or deity.

God has appointed to each creature a place in His ordered universe. Authority and submission are essential to that order. Since God has given to man the place of authority, we must accept the place He has given to women, with its responsibilities and privileges—and accept it with gladness, knowing that submission (in God's wise design) is for us the means of blessing and fulfillment. We are to function uniquely, according to God's design. Are we willing to let God be God?

THE COVERED HEAD

1 Corinthians 11:3-16, which teaches headship, indicates that this principle is to be *manifested* in the church by the wearing of a head-covering, a veil, by the women. J. B. Nicholson writes: "When a man appears with head covered, or a woman with head uncovered, it is an implicit denial of the divine teaching regarding headship." He explains this by saying that man represents God and is the glory of God; that God's authority must be unchallenged and His glory must not be hid; that therefore a man's head must be uncovered as he fulfills his spiritual functions in the church. At the same time, the "woman is the glory of the man" and this glory must *not* be manifested, so the woman is to be covered—that God alone may be glorified.

Is the covering a woman's hair? Some say that it is, but we notice that a different word is used for covering in the original language in verse 15 relating to hair, from the word used in verses 4-7 of a covering one could put on or off. The covering required in these verses is obviously not hair, or else only a bald man could function! (see verse 4).

When are women expected to wear a head covering? There is no general agreement on this, but it would seem to us that the head should be covered in a church gathering when men are present.

Was this requirement intended only to fit local circumstances of that day, or is it applicable to women today? Note the basis of Paul's arguments: 1) Headship is God's arrangement, not man's (11:3); 2) it is based on creation order—it did not arise from local custom, either

Jewish or Greek. Man was created first; the woman was created for the man (11:8, 9). Therefore this requirement is fundamental, unaltered by varying circumstances of place or time. Headship is an abiding principle, so the recognition and manifestation of submission *is* enjoined on us today if we are to please God.

Rebekah took a veil and covered herself on meeting Isaac (Genesis 24:65-67). This was a significant rite in marriage, indicating that the woman's husband was now her head. The head covering—veil or hat—does not carry the same significance of submission in today's culture, at least in the West. But in the absence of other means of expressing subjection, should not the Christian woman who wants to please the Lord be glad to show in this way her submission of heart *to the Lord?* God grant us the grace of submission that we may show to men and to angels the meek and quiet spirit that is so precious to God.

FURTHER STUDY

Obtain a copy and read "The Place of Women in the Church." (Refer to bibliography at the end of the course for further details.)

MEMORY VERSE ASSIGNMENT

Memorize 1 Corinthians 11:3

[1]Gary Inrig, *Life in His Body* (Harold Shaw Publishers, Wheaton, Illinois), page 161.

When you have mastered this lesson, take the first part of Exam 4 (covering Lesson 7), questions 1-10 on pages 79-80 (right after Lesson 8).

LESSON 7

PERSONAL QUESTIONS TO PONDER

1) Do I clearly understand that the spiritual equality of men and women in their standing before God—*and* differences in their functions—are both taught in the Bible?

_____

_____

_____

_____

2) Is my spiritual condition and my ministry important to the well-being of my local church? Am I really needed? Would I be missed?

_____

_____

_____

_____

3) Do I understand the meaning of the head-covering?

_____

_____

_____

_____

Pray that God will help you clearly understand *your* standing before Him, that your spiritual condition and ministry will be to the well-being of your local church, that you will be submissive to God's way.

MY PERSONAL PRAYER

_____

_____

_____

_____

_____

_____

_____

_____

_____

LESSON EIGHT

Further Instructions to Women

INSTRUCTIONS TO WIVES

At this point it might be well to mention three other passages that deal with subjection. These are addressed specifically to wives. "Wives, submit yourselves unto your own husbands, as unto the Lord. For the husband is the head of the wife, even as Christ is head of the church and He is the Savior of the body. Therefore as the church is subject unto Christ, so let the wives be to their own husbands in everything" (Ephesians 5:22-24). See also Colossians 3:18. Note that the injunction is, "submit yourselves," indicating a voluntary acceptance of this position. And the following verses (25-33) impose a very heavy burden of responsibility on husbands—"Husbands, love your wives, *even as Christ* also loved the church and gave himself for it...." God has charged the husband with loving headship; He charges the wife to help him fulfill his responsibility—not to make it hard for him. Subjection of wives to husbands, as the Church is subject to Christ, is an important part of the Church's message. It is a beautiful illustration of divine truth.

In 1 Peter 3:1-4 we read: "Ye wives, be in subjection to your own husbands; that, if any obey not the word, they also may without the word be won by the conversation of the wives; while they behold your chaste conversation (manner of life) coupled with fear. Whose adorning let it not be that outward adorning of plaiting the hair, and of wearing of gold, or of putting on of apparel; but let it be the hidden man of the heart, in that which is not corruptible, even the ornament of a meek and quiet spirit, which is in the sight of God of great price."

While these instructions are given to wives, they reveal the kind of woman who pleases God, whether married or single. Surely a chaste manner of life, with stress not on outward adornment but rather on beauty of character, is what we all should seek after. The precious quality of a quiet and gentle spirit seems far removed from the self-assertion, the strident voices and the aggressiveness seen in some of today's women. We are exhorted not to let the world press us into its mold, but to be transformed by the renewing of our minds (Romans 12:2). Submission does not come easily to any of us; the natural human behavior is self-assertion. But we are called to exhibit the supernatural—the very life of Christ "who ... made Himself of no reputation ... and humbled Himself ... even to the death of the cross" ... for our sakes (Philippians 2:5-8). How better could we show the life of Christ in us—make Him visible to the world around—than by following His example of submission? He said, "Take my yoke upon you and learn of Me, for I am *meek and lowly in heart*" (Matthew 11:29).

Again, we emphasize that submission does not denote inferiority or weakness but rather strength of character. "He that ruleth his spirit (is better) than he that taketh a city" (Proverbs 16:32).

One last word here on submission. Obviously this privilege is not meant only for wives, or for all women, but for all Christians. Paul writes: "Be filled with the Spirit ... submitting yourselves one to another in the fear of God" (Ephesians 5:21). See also 1 Peter 5:5. A submissive heart should characterize every believer, first in recognizing the Lordship of Christ over all of life, and then in laying down life in service for others (1 John 3:16).

Christian women don't need to draw attention to themselves by outward adornment, or to seek "status" by public activities. Conscious of their relationship to Christ and their worth in His eyes, they have an inner dignity and beauty. The heathen world took note of this modesty and simplicity in the early Christian women and contrasted it with the extravagances and immoralities of heathen women.

One pagan, Libanius, remarked, "What women these Christians have!"

PRINCIPLE OF SILENCE (1 Corinthians 14:34, 35; 1 Timothy 2:11-15)

Linked to the principle of headship and submission, is the principle of women's silence in the church gatherings. Paul writes: "Let the woman learn in silence with all subjection ... I suffer not a woman to teach, nor to usurp authority over the man, but to be in silence" (1 Timothy 2:11, 12).

The specific prohibition is that women should not teach men nor have authority over them in church affairs. And the reasons are given: "For Adam was first formed, then Eve. And Adam was not deceived, but the woman being deceived was in the transgression" (1 Timothy 2:13, 14). The apostle Paul here appeals to creation order and to the Fall as the basis of the requirement for women's silence—not to any cultural or local situation of the first century. This is basic ground and therefore the requirement is binding for us today. (Note, too, that in 1 Timothy 2:8 Paul restricts public praying to males.)

Paul also wrote to the believers at Corinth: "Let your women keep silence in the churches: for it is not permitted unto them to speak; but they are commanded to be under obedience ... It is a shame for women to speak in the church" (1 Corinthians 14:34, 35). Some contend that Paul is here forbidding the chatter or gossip of women during a service, but the word translated "speak" does not mean to chatter. The same word is used of God in verse 21.

Notice that this whole 14th chapter is dealing with *order* in church gatherings and the edifying of the church (verses 4, 5, 12, 19, 23, 33)—regulating such matters as the use of tongues and the ministry of prophets, as well as giving instructions to women. It is in this connection, then, that the proper behavior of women is clearly stated: they are not permitted to speak and they are commanded to be under obedience. Their subjection would be nullified by public speaking. The uniform testimony of the New Testament is that while women have many valuable ministries, it is not given to them to have a public ministry in the church. Indeed, they are not permitted even to ask questions publicly in the church (verse 35). E. W. Rogers writes: "The whole controversy as to women's place is based on an exaggerated notion of the importance of platform ministry. Every servant of God knows that prayer is more important than preaching and this is exactly what sisters can do, perhaps better than men."

Note that Paul says, "the things that I write unto you are the commandments of the *Lord*" (verse 37). This includes all that has been dealt with previously, including the instructions about women. These are not just Paul's ideas!

We cannot leave this subject of women's silence without reference to what is said in 1 Corinthians 11:5—"But every woman that prayeth or prophesieth with her head uncovered, dishonoreth her head." *Were* women praying and prophesying in public? Is Paul *permitting* public ministry for women in 1 Corinthians 11 and *forbidding* it in 1 Corinthians 14? Hardly! Much has been written from every possible viewpoint about the meaning and significance of this verse. May we just point out that the subject under consideration in chapter 11 is headship and subjection, not church order. Paul is not dealing here with the question of whether or not women should speak in public. When that subject does come up, in the sections where he deals with order in the church (1 Corinthians 14 and 1 Timothy 2), there can be no question as to his teaching—silence is clearly commanded. What then does he mean by this reference to women praying and prophesying in 1 Corinthians 11? We are driven to the conclusion that if women were praying and prophesying in public in Corinth, it was extraordinary; this was not the custom in other churches (1 Corinthians 11:16) but was unique to Corinth, a church that had numerous irregularities. The principle of silence clearly taught in 1 Corinthians 14 and 1 Timothy 2 is based on the teaching of headship and subjection in 1 Corinthians 11, and is not altered by the incidental reference to the irregular activities of women in Corinth.

MEMORY VERSE ASSIGNMENT
Memorize 1 Timothy 2:11-12

When you are ready, complete Exam 4 by answering questions 11-20 on pages 81-82. (You should have already answered questions 1-10 as part of your study of Lesson 7.)

LESSON 8

PERSONAL QUESTIONS TO PONDER

(Write out your answers to these questions. You may, if you wish, submit your answers to your instructor for comment and evaluation.)

1) As a wife, am I making it hard for my husband to fulfill his responsibility as head of the home?

_____

_____

_____

2) As a woman, do I strive for beauty of character and a quiet, gentle spirit—or do I seek attention by outward adornment, aggressiveness, witty remarks, personal accomplishments?

_____

_____

_____

3) Does the injunction that women are to be silent in church leave me feeling rebellious? If so, ask the Lord's help. He may show you a deep desire for self-exaltation and indulgence that needs to be dealt with.

_____

_____

_____

_____

_____

Pray that you will be able to make it easy for your husband to fulfill his responsibilities as head of the home; pray for beauty of character and for a quiet, gentle spirit; pray for the removal of any rebelliousness, self-exaltation and indulgence.

MY PERSONAL PRAYER

_____

_____

_____

_____

_____

_____

_____

THE WOMAN WHO PLEASES GOD

Exam 4
Lessons 7 and 8

Name _____ Exam Grade _____
(print plainly)

Address_____

City_____ State _____ Zip Code_____ Class Number _____

Instructor _____

LESSON 7

In the blank space in the right-hand margin write the letter of the correct answer. (50 points)

1. The Apostle Paul clearly states that
   a. women are inferior to men
   b. women have the same standing before God as men do
   c. women should function in the church in the same way as men
   d. the ministry of women is not important   _____

2. We are "all the children of God by faith in Christ Jesus."
   a. This negates all differences between Jews and Gentiles
   b. This negates all differences between slaves and freemen
   c. This negates all differences between males and females
   d. This does not alter sexual differences   _____

3. God designed the sexual differences at Creation because
   a. man was to be superior to woman
   b. variety is better than uniformity
   c. He had different functions in mind for the man and the woman
   d. He was experimenting as He went along   _____

4. In the New Testament we see women
   a. among the Lord's twelve disciples
   b. at the institution of the Lord's Supper
   c. as writers of some of the epistles
   d. enduring persecution for Christ's sake along with men   _____

5. The principles of headship and submission
  a. are evident throughout the Bible
  b. were first stated at the giving of the law
  c. were introduced by the Apostle Paul
  d. do not apply in our culture   _____

6. From memory quote I Corinthians 11:3

  " _____

  _____

  _____ "

7. The principle of headship
  a. downgrades woman because she is last in the order
  b. shows the order of authority and submission
  c. cannot be shown in the church today
  d. glorifies man and should be rejected by woman   _____

8. The teaching for women to wear a head covering in church gatherings
  a. came from a Jewish custom
  b. came from a Greek custom
  c. was based on the order of creation of man and woman
  d. was not recognized in most of the early churches   _____

9. The head covering—veil or hat—
  a. is not a symbol of submission to most people today in the West
  b. is still a recognized symbol of submission in our society
  c. was never part of the ritual of marriage
  d. is not needed if a woman has long hair   _____

10. The Christian woman who covers her head in church
  a. shows in this way her submission of heart to the Lord
  b. is observed with approval by the angels
  c. pleases the Lord by her obedience
  d. does all of the above   _____

WHAT DO YOU SAY?

Is it important to you to be the kind of woman who pleases God? If so, what should be your response to the teaching about submission given in this lesson?

_____

_____

_____

_____

_____

LESSON 8

In the blank space in the right-hand margin write the letter of the correct answer. (50 points)

11. The New Testament teaches that wives
   a. are to be compelled to submit to their husbands' control
   b. are to submit themselves to their own husbands
   c. are inferior to their husbands
   d. should stand up for their rights   _____

12. Husbands are charged to love their wives
   a. as Christ loved the church
   b. as they love and cherish their own bodies
   c. as they love themselves
   d. in all of the above ways   _____

13. Christian women should stress and seek after
   a. intellectual development
   b. beauty in dress
   c. development of a meek and quiet spirit
   d. opportunities for self-expression   _____

14. Submission
   a. comes easily to most people
   b. is part of natural human behavior
   c. was exemplified for us by the Lord Jesus
   d. implies inferiority   _____

15. Submission is required
   a. only of wives
   b. only of women, not men
   c. only of those who are weak
   d. of all believers   _____

16. From memory quote I Timothy 2:11-12

"_____

_____

_____

_____"

17. The principle of women's silence in church gatherings
   a. is based on the order of creation and the Fall
   b. is based on Jewish custom
   c. comes from Greek culture
   d. applied only to first century churches   _____

18. The word translated "speak" in 1 Corinthians 14:34 really meant
   a. chattering
   b. gossiping
   c. speaking in a public service
   d. speaking in tongues   _____

19. Instructions concerning women's silence in the church
   a. were the idea of the Apostle Paul
   b. were given by command of the Lord
   c. were not followed by most of the early churches
   d. need not be heeded today   _____

20. Women apparently prayed and prophesied in Corinth. This was
   a. permitted by the Apostle Paul
   b. all right as long as they covered their heads
   c. a situation unique to Corinth
   d. the custom in all the churches   _____

WHAT DO YOU SAY?

What really is your priority—outward adornment, intellectualism, self-expression, or the development of a meek and quiet spirit?

_____

_____

_____

_____

Women in the Home

RELATIONSHIP TO HUSBAND

We have already considered the relationship of husband and wife in Ephesians 5:22 and 25. "Wives, submit yourselves unto your own husbands as unto the Lord.... Husbands, love your wives, even as Christ also loved the church and gave himself for it." Two other passages exhort wives to submit to their husbands—Colossians 3:18 and 1 Peter 3:1. What does it mean to submit? The dictionary says— "to yield oneself to the authority or will of another." Is this demeaning to the wife? No, it is simply God's order, designed for the good of humanity.

Male-female differences, as ordained by God, are important, and the present drive to nullify them is a threat to marriage and to society, for marriage is basic to a sound society. God's order for the wife is submission, not servility; for the husband, authority modeled on Christ who "gave Himself." The ideal is loving consideration for one another and mutual respect. This attitude is promoted by a spirit of openness and sharing. The husband and wife who have the same life goal—of living to please the Lord—and who regularly read the Bible and pray together as "heirs together of the grace of life," will have little trouble with the concepts of submission and authority. When both are yielded to the Lord, all other relationships will fall into their proper places. True Christian marriage is the union of a man and a woman, equal in worth, complementing each other in function, in harmony with one another because God has first place in both of their lives.

In the case of a couple where the husband is failing to fulfill his duty as given in Ephesians 5:25, the wife is still to be obedient to her duty of Ephesians 5:22. Likewise, if the wife fails in her part, the husband should still be faithful to his. The duty of each is clear; one is not dependent on the other. The command to each is plain and should be carried out in obedience to the Lord, regardless of the other's conduct.

Someone has said, "If the husband wants to be treated like a king, he should treat his wife like a queen. If he treats his wife like a queen, she will have no difficulty in treating him like a king." There should be mutual respect (Ephesians 5:33; 1 Peter 3:7), mutual consideration in marital relations (1 Corinthians 7:3-5), and a recognition of interdependence (1 Corinthians 11:8-12).

The wife must carry out her responsibilities of running the home as faithfully as she expects her husband to attend to his daily employment. Proverbs 14:1 says, "Every wise woman buildeth her house." Taking the stuff of your life and shaping it creatively is a challenge. True, there are many routine, less-pleasant tasks in homemaking, but no work is menial. We're enjoined to work with our hands (1 Thessalonians 4:11; Ephesians 4:28). Our Lord did it, and the Apostle Paul. Doing things with love, giving of ourselves without grudging, will lighten any task.

RELATIONSHIP TO CHILDREN

It is no small responsibility to be a godly wife and mother. While a child will get his view of God from both parents, the mother's influence is especially great in the early years of life. The pre-school years are formative, and the importance of godly teaching and example cannot be over-stressed. We have seen this exemplified in the sons of Jochebed and Hannah.

We are increasingly being made aware of the importance of *love* to the full development of babies and young children. Yet our news is all too often full of tragic stories about battered or neglected children; of abortion on demand; of sad, unwanted children. Surely, as Christian women, we should pour out our love, not only on our own

84

children, but on all with whom we come in contact—particularly those who have special needs. "Whosoever shall receive one of such children in my name, receiveth Me," said the Lord Jesus (Matthew 10:42 and Mark 9:37).

In our day, when so many women work outside the home, we do well to stop and examine this practice. In a case of economic necessity—and there are many such—no question need be raised. But when a mother works solely to be able to get some "extras" for the family or the house, to secure a "higher" standard of living, she should be very sure that she is not losing more than she gains. No babysitter or day nursery can fully take the mother's place in loving and training a child. The pre-school days are precious and all too few, and the mother should have time to take her child for walks and begin to develop in him an appreciation of nature; to read to him and sing and pray; to play games and fly kites; to share his excitement over daily discoveries in the world around; to teach him the difference between right and wrong; to show him he is an important person made by God and of value to God. Those early days of sharing are necessary if communication is to be preserved into and through the teen years. Whenever possible, the mother should be at home when the children are at home.

Someone has said, "Home should have a loving smell"—of cookies and bread baking! Home should be a place of comfort and love, of warmth and welcome—a place of beauty, for love helps us to do things beautifully. What kind of memories of home will our children carry through life? Home-making can be the most creative and satisfying occupation any woman could want.

A most important part of a mother's work is the *training* and discipline of her children. This is a mutual responsibility of mother and father, but most fathers are not at home during the day, so much of the burden necessarily falls on the mother. Her guide must be the Word of God, and it is only by prayer and dependence on the Lord that she is enabled for this responsibility.

Deuteronomy 6:6, 7 says: "And these words, which I command thee this day, shall be *in thine heart:* and thou shalt *teach them diligently* unto thy children, and shall talk of them when thou sittest in thine house, and when thou walkest by the way, and when thou liest down, and when thou risest up." These were instructions given to Israel by Moses, but they're just as applicable today. The Word must be *first* in *our* hearts. "Let the word of Christ dwell in you richly" (Colossians 3:16). No mother can afford to miss her Quiet Time with the Lord, reading the Word and praying day by day. And what a privilege it is to teach our children about the Lord. This should begin in babyhood and should be a natural part of daily living—talking about God while sitting in the house, walking outdoors, at bedtime and in the morning, as Deuteronomy 6 suggests. There should also be a time each day when the whole family reads the Bible together and prays. This could be at breakfast, or at dinner, or any suitable time, but it should be a regular part of the family schedule, carefully planned and observed.

Discipline is a word we shrink from, but it's really only the setting of boundaries for our children. Punishment results if the child deliberately goes beyond the boundaries. Knowing the rules, and knowing that disobedience will be punished consistently, gives a child a sense of security. Ephesians 6:4 says, "Provoke not your children to wrath." (Don't scold and nag and make them angry and resentful.) We must carefully formulate our own Christian values and standards for the family, then teach them to our children until they begin of themselves to make the right choices on the basis of what they have learned. This is our goal for them.

Above all, we should *pray* for our children. We have the example in this of Abraham (Genesis 17:18) and David (1 Chronicles 29:19). We are warned against showing partiality, loving one child more than another, by the sad examples of Isaac and Rebekah (Genesis 25:28), and Jacob (Genesis 37:3), and the disruption of home life that followed. We are also warned against indulgence and failure to correct our children by the tragic results in Eli's household, where God's judgment fell "because his sons made themselves vile, and he restrained them not" (1 Samuel 3:13).

NEIGHBORS

The influence of a Christian home should go beyond the walls of that home. Is our manner of life no different from that of our neighbors? Or do they see in our family something that they lack and would like to have? The atmosphere of a genuine Christian home might be a wholly new thing to your children's friends as they come and go, and to your neighbors who drop in. A happy, united family in a loving home is not common these days.

The first part of this lesson, relating to wives and mothers, does not concern the single woman, but single women have a home of some kind—and neighbors to whom they can show the love of Christ. Genuine friendship is always appreciated, and a readiness to help and serve others.

CHARACTER AND CLOTHING

Two passages which speak of a Christian woman's character are 1 Timothy 3:11 and Titus 2:3-5. A summary of the adjectives listed there would include dignified, sober-minded, self-controlled, dependable, loving, trustworthy and chaste.

As for clothing, 1 Peter 3:3, 4 stresses, not outward adornment, but rather beauty of spirit. 1 Timothy 2:9, 10 calls for modest dress, not showy and attracting undue attention to ourselves. Let us seek in this matter, as in all others, to be pleasing to God. Let us be careful to give more time to developing the inner beauty of character than that we give to adorning our bodies.

USE OF THE HOME FOR THE LORD

Hospitality is a ministry that is valued highly by the Lord and His people (1 Peter 4:9; Hebrews 13:2). It's not necessary to have a large, well-equipped house and to make lavish provision; a single person living in one room can show hospitality. A loving welcome and simple food will give pleasure, and the single women who practice hospitality have by far the richest lives.

Christian service can be carried on in the home. Here are some suggestions:

1. Children's clubs. Many children have been won for the Lord through home children's clubs. Those who feel they cannot teach can offer the use of their homes for one afternoon a week and help the teacher in various ways.
2. Women's coffee hours. These have proved very effective, both in reaching the unsaved and in helping young Christians to grow. Again, those who feel they can't teach can open their homes, invite their neighbors in, supply the coffee, and support in prayer the one who is leading the group.
3. Couples' study groups. Several couples, who meet in an evening

for Bible study and sharing, will grow together in knowledge of the Word and often will develop deep and lasting friendships.

4. Other activities. Perhaps some feel unable to give time for such ministries as the above. There are other things to do in a home, such as a) telephoning someone who is ill or alone; b) making cookies or casseroles to help out a family or friend in need (or just to say "I love you" in a practical way); c) using a skill such as sewing or knitting to make things for others; d) writing letters to missionaries and shut-ins (to say nothing of family and friends); e) praying! This last is the greatest ministry of all and perhaps the most neglected. But "whatsoever ye do, do *all* to the glory of God" (1 Corinthians 10:31).

When you have mastered this lesson, take the first part of Exam 5 (covering Lesson 9), questions 1-10 on pages 101-102 (right after Lesson 10).

LESSON 9

PERSONAL QUESTIONS TO PONDER

(Write out your answers to these questions. You may, if you wish, submit your answers to your instructor for comment and evaluation.)

1) Do I feel I am being unfairly put down when I read, "Wives, submit..."?

_____

_____

_____

_____

2) Have I tried doing some of my household duties creatively to-day?

_____

_____

_____

_____

3) If I work outside the home, have I carefully thought through just what I gain and what I lose? Is it worthwhile in view of the personal and spiritual needs of my family? Is it just as "escape" for me from home duties I dislike?

_____

_____

_____

_____

4) Have I had a quiet time with God today? Have I prayed earnestly for my husband and children?

_____

_____

_____

_____

5) How can I use my home for the Lord? Is there something I can do today?

_____

_____

_____

_____

Pray that God will help you to submissively respond to the teachings of Scripture; that He will help you do some of your household duties creatively; that He will help you think through your real motives for working outside the home; that He will help you re-arrange your day so that you can have a quiet time with Him; that He will help you pray earnestly for your husband, children and family; that He will help you use your home for His glory.

MY PERSONAL PRAYER

_____

_____

Women's Ministry Outside the Home

IN BUSINESS AND PROFESSIONAL LIFE

In our last lesson we mentioned some ways in which women can serve God in their homes. There are opportunities, too, for those in secular employment to witness effectively for Him. Their witness will be primarily the impact of their whole manner of life—their personalities, attitudes, interests—which will open the way for the spoken witness if they are alert to opportunities. In whatever situation we find ourselves we can shine for the Lord. Care must be taken not to use our employer's time for witnessing; we should perform faithfully and honestly the work for which we are being paid. Paul wrote to the Christians at Colosse that they should work "not with the idea of currying favor [when others are watching], but as a sincere expression of your devotion to the Lord; put your whole heart and soul into it as if working for the Lord" (Colossians 3:22, 23).

IN THE CHURCH

In connection with the local church, women's ministry is of great value. They normally carry the main burden of children's work in Sunday school and Vacation Bible School, conduct women's gospel meetings and Bible studies, carry on missionary prayer and work groups, help with music, and spend many hours visiting the sick and helping those in need—spiritually as well as in a material way. Much of the warmth that welcomes visitors to our churches comes from women whose hearts God has touched. What a help it is to the men who bear the responsibility of guiding and teaching the church to have the encouragement and prayer support (and presence!) of the women. Our attitudes and spiritual condition are *not* unimportant, even though our voices are not heard in public gatherings. We are one body, and the condition of every part affects the whole. Needless to say, the women's contribution to the fellowship aspect of church life is important and much appreciated, but it is not their only contribution. There is plenty of scope for the exercise of women's spiritual gifts within the framework of church order as set forth by the Apostle Paul. A supportive ministry is essential to the functioning and well-being of the church, just as an army requires about ten men working behind the lines for every front-line soldier. And who is to say which one is more important? What higher honor could we have than to be called a servant of the church, a succorer of many, a helper in Christ Jesus (Romans 16:1-3)?

ON THE MISSION FIELD

Our particular focus in this lesson is the place of women on the mission field—a sphere in which women have played a large part over the years. From the morning of the resurrection when Mary Magdalene was told to "Go and tell' what she had seen and heard (John 20:17, 18), women have been witnessing for their Lord. The beginning of the 19th century saw the first woman missionaries going from the West to foreign lands. The names of some are well-known (e.g., Mary Slessor, Amy Carmichael, Malla Moe), but thousands whose names are unknown to us have done what God sent them to do, making their valuable contribution with quiet devotion to the Lord.

1. How do I know?

The first question that comes to our minds is, How do I know if

God wants me to be a missionary? Much has been written on the subject of how to know the will of God, and it would be impossible to start such a discussion here. Someone has said, "The difficulty we have in knowing God's will is the measure of our distance from Him." The believer who is consciously walking with the Lord, humbly wanting His will day by day, wholly yielded to Him to obey in all things—such a believer will know the Lord's leading step by step. Too many of us would like a whole blueprint of what God has in mind for us, but that is not His way. He leads us a step at a time and usually reveals to us the second step only after the first has been taken. *"As thou goest,* step by step, I will open up the way before thee."

2. How do I prepare?

Our primary responsibility as Christians is to know the Lord in His Word and in experience. There is no substitute for daily meditation and regular study of the Bible, for God has revealed Himself in His Word. This is not something for missionaries only, or for men only; mothers and secretaries, teachers and factory workers, all of us who want to please God will give time and attention to what He has said.

Before His ascension the Lord said to His disciples: "Ye shall be my witnesses..." (Acts 1:8). Since a witness can only tell what he himself has seen and heard and experienced, we must have some knowledge and experience of the Lord to share with others. A newborn Christian can share the joy of sins forgiven, but a missionary must know more than that. Missionaries should be equipped to teach and nurture those whom they lead to Christ, to see them firmly established in the faith and growing into strong and fruitful Christians, able to withstand temptation and to survive the persecution and opposition that so often follow conversion to Christ.

In other words, before a person can *do* the work of a missionary, she must *be* a person in whose life God has been working. To such an one comes the call of the Lord. He calls us to a place in His program—perhaps at home, perhaps overseas. Our sex, age, education, social standing are not of primary importance, and not for us to worry about. The Lord who knows us through and through is the One who assigns our place as He sees best. And He does not call us to a task without enabling us for it.

3. Are missionaries needed?

Many are raising the question today—"Are missionaries still needed in today's world?" The answer is an unqualified Yes! Until the Lord Jesus returns for His people, the Great Commission (Matthew 28:18-20) is binding upon us. The Lord Jesus said, "Go ... and lo, I am with you."

But haven't conditions changed, and aren't many countries closed to missionaries? Again, Yes. But there are still many open doors, and the sovereign Lord is the one who opens and closes doors (Revelation 3:7). He is in control of the world situation, even though at times it may not seem so to us.

4. Ministries today

At the present time missionary women are engaged in a variety of ministries in the world. Some are directly evangelistic; others are "handmaids to the gospel."

a. Medical. Perhaps nothing has opened doors for the gospel as readily as medical work. The Lord Jesus Himself went about healing, and the loving concern shown by missionary nurses and doctors has demonstrated the love of God and often made people willing to listen to the gospel. In countries where extensive medical work has been carried on in the past, national governments are now taking over the health care of their people, but many rural areas in the world still need missionary medical personnel. In Muslim areas where women are isolated in their homes away from men, women doctors and nurses are doing a great work. Medical workers are still serving and are still in demand in parts of Africa, Asia, and Latin America.

b. Educational. In the early days of missions, day schools were an integral part of the work, for it was necessary that the Christians be taught to read so that they could read the Bible for themselves. Mission schools were the *only* schools in many areas. Now many national governments are taking over the school systems, but, happily, missionaries are still permitted to teach the Scriptures in many of these government-sponsored schools. Then there are the schools for missionaries' children which must be staffed. These require qualified teachers with credentials such as those needed for teaching at home. Some missionaries teach Domestic Science classes and Home Economics. Practically all missionaries are involved in teaching of some kind—in Sunday school and Bible classes. In view of this, it would be helpful to all outgoing missionaries to have studied some courses in Christian Education.

c. Literature. There are many facets to a literature ministry, beginning with a study of linguistics and getting an unwritten language down on paper. Then comes translation work, putting the Bible and other literature into the new language. Then the literacy classes, when people are taught to read. There is writing and editing to be done, printing and publishing, then distribution of literature by bookstore, bookmobile, mail and personal contact. Women are involved in all of these tasks. Emmaus Correspondence courses form a large part of the literature ministry of many missionaries, and office skills are invaluable in handling the courses. Literature is an excellent means of spreading the gospel, by going into the inaccessible areas and countries closed to missionaries, but it cannot replace the personal contact of the missionary entirely. The sacrificial, self-giving of the worker—the face-to-face encounter—are still the most effective way of winning people to Christ.

d. Camps. Those who have had experience in camp work at home will realize the value of this ministry. Missionaries, too, are finding that camp work is really fruitful and are expanding their outreach in many areas.

e. Other ministries. These would include 1) secretarial work— very much needed in connection with hospitals, publishing and printing, any kind of institution; 2) helping to produce radio programs; 3) running orphanages or youth hostels, or serving as a dorm mother; 4) work among university students; 5) doing art work and lay-outs for printers; 6) hospitality for other missionaries or for state officials. The list could go on and on! Whatever gift or training we have, no matter how small, can be used by the Lord if yielded to Him.

"Live life, then, with a due sense of responsibility, not as those who do not know the meaning and purpose of life, but as those who do. Make the best use of your time, despite all the difficulties of these days. Don't be vague, but firmly grasp what you know to be the will of God" (Ephesians 5:15-17, Phillips).

When you are ready, complete Exam 5 by answering questions 11-20 on pages 103-104. (You should have already answered questions 1-10 as part of your study of Lesson 9.)

LESSON 10

PERSONAL QUESTIONS TO PONDER

(Write out your answers to these questions. You may, if you wish, submit your answers to your instructor for comment and evaluation.)

1) If I am employed, what kind of opinion does my employer have of me?

_____

_____

_____

_____

2) How am I contributing to my church? Do I make an effort to speak to visitors? Do I offer to help when volunteers are needed? Do I show love and care for others?

_____

_____

_____

_____

3) Do I pray for any missionaries by name, knowing their needs and problems? Do I keep informed about world needs and opportunities for service?

_____

_____

_____

4) Have I opened myself to God so that He may show me where He would like me to serve Him?

_____

_____

_____

Pray that your employment will be to the glory of God; that you will make the maximum contribution to your church; that you will develop an increasing interest in missions and missionaries; that you will serve God in the field and sphere of His choice.

MY PERSONAL PRAYER

_____

_____

_____

_____

_____

_____

THE WOMAN WHO PLEASES GOD

Exam
Name _____ Grade _____
(print plainly)

Address_____

City_____ State _____ Zip Code _____ Class Number _____

Instructor _____

LESSON 9

In the blank space in the right-hand margin write the letter of the correct answer. (50 points)

1. The call for wives to submit to their husbands
   a. is demeaning to women
   b. puts wives on the level of servants
   c. gives husbands the right to be boss in the home
   d. is part of God's wise design and meant for blessing   _____

2. A mother should work outside the home if she wants to,
   a. if it's an economic necessity
   b. to raise the standard of living for her family
   c. so she can hire someone else to do household work
   d. because others can care for her children as well as she
       can   _____

3. The work of running a home
   a. is mostly drudgery
   b. is too menial for an educated woman
   c. gives no outlet for creative ability
   d. can be enjoyable if done with love, not grudgingly   _____

4. The influence of mothers on young children
   a. has been greatly over-rated
   b. cannot be overstressed
   c. is nowhere shown in the Bible
   d. is quickly forgotten as they grow older   _____

5. The work of teaching and training children
   a. falls largely on the father
   b. should be left to school and church
   c. is a privilege to a mother who knows the Lord
   d. need not begin until the child is of school age   _____

6. We have a good example of parent-child relationship in the lives of
   a. Abraham-Isaac
   b. Rebekah-Jacob and Esau
   c. Jacob-Joseph
   d. Eli-Hophni and Phineas

7. According to the letters to Timothy and Titus, a Christian woman should be
   a. aggressive
   b. dynamic
   c. serious
   d. attractive

8. The Christian woman should not be characterized by
   a. fancy hair-dos
   b. costly clothing
   c. jewelry
   d. any of the above

9. Hospitality
   a. is a ministry for rich people only
   b. requires a good-sized home
   c. is a responsibility of all Christians
   d. is not mentioned in the Bible

10. The greatest ministry a Christian woman can engage in is
   a. teaching
   b. prayer
   c. hospitality
   d. letter-writing

WHAT DO YOU SAY?

Is your home a place of warmth and welcome for the Lord and His people?

_____

_____

_____

_____

_____

LESSON 10

In the blank space in the right-hand margin write the letter of the correct answer. (50 points)

11. The Christian in secular employment should
    a. talk and act just like fellow-workers
    b. constantly be witnessing for the Lord at work
    c. work whole-heartedly during business hours
    d. not try to win fellow-workers to Christ at all   _____

12. Women's ministry in the local church is
    a. confined to teaching children
    b. largely in connection with social affairs
    c. forbidden by the Apostle Paul
    d. a supportive ministry essential to the functioning of the church   _____

13. God makes His will known to us
    a. step by step as we walk with Him
    b. in a complete blueprint for our lives
    c. by dreams and visions
    d. when we're too busy to listen to Him   _____

14. A prospective missionary must
    a. know his sins are forgiven
    b. be able to teach and nurture others in the Christian life
    c. engage in daily Bible study to know God's Word
    d. do all of the above   _____

15. To go out as a missionary, one should
    a. be under thirty years of age
    b. be a graduate of college and/or Bible school
    c. be yielded to the Lord to go where He sends
    d. be all of the above   _____

16. Which of the following statements is true?
    a. "The day of missions is over"
    b. "Missionaries are no longer needed"
    c. "Mission churches no longer want missionaries"
    d. "The Great Commission is still in effect today"   _____

17. Missionary medical work is being carried on today in
    a. Poland
    b. Pakistan
    c. France
    d. Jamaica   _____

18. All missionaries should
   a.   run day schools for the nationals
   b.   teach the Bible
   c.   have teaching certificates
   d.   leave school teaching to the government   _____

19. Christian literature is a most effective means of spreading the gospel. Which of the following things is it **NOT** able to do?
   a.   It can go into countries which are closed to missionaries
   b.   It can reach isolated areas inaccessible to missionaries
   c.   It can replace the need for personal missionary work
   d.   It can repeat its message over and over again   _____

20 In addition to medical, educational and literature ministries, list five areas in which women are presently involved on the mission field.

_____

_____

WHAT DO YOU SAY?

Have you presented yourself to the Lord to do His will wherever He might lead you? Read Romans 12:1, 2 prayerfully before you answer.

_____

_____

_____

_____

_____

False and True Liberty

It seems that there are two main groups holding a feminist position, each of which attempts to define the role of the woman as she relates to society, to the work-a-day world, and to her family.

The non-Christian feminist largely ignores the Biblical perspective. Historically, the abolitionist and suffragette periods would be considered by most as the beginning of the movement for women's liberation. Primary purposes were to gain rights for slaves, and then for women, equal to those enjoyed by men, especially in the political sphere—namely, the privilege of voting. Once this was secured, there was the drive to gain equality in education and professional opportunities. Proponents of this liberation movement reasoned that some women were as intelligent as some men, and being endowed with comparable intelligence, they wanted opportunities to develop and use it. Several factors combined to help the feminist position in this area. Jobs, left vacant when men were called into military service, were capably filled by women. The economic crunch called for a second income to help meet family needs. Some creative women began to express themselves in the arts (sometimes under an alias to secure publication). Political pressure was gradually brought to bear upon law-makers.

As the movement gained in popularity, other areas of life were re-evaluated, including the role of the working wife. The women reasoned, "If I work as many hours as my husband, I am just as tired as he is when he comes home from his job, so we should share in home chores." Thus, the husband was expected to share equally in shopping, meal preparation, child care, housecleaning, etc. This led to the concept of egalitarian marriages—an equal sharing of decisions and responsibilities, with little differentiation in the functions of husband and wife. The patriarchal home concept was too "limited" for the liberated woman: she was now free to seek the kind of employment she wanted; she was liberated from the role of house-wife. Words like "male chauvinist" began to be used—to designate the men who supposedly put down women and wanted to restrict them to the home sphere.

Some of the feminist objectives *are* desirable. For example, most of us would agree that equal pay should be received for equal work, whether done by a male or by a female. Just as appealing to many was the aim to dignify the position of women.

The Christian feminist picks up many of the issues of the secular movement, but seeks to find Scriptural backing for the position taken. Some assert that Scripture supports the thesis of women's equality with men; they quote certain passages of their choosing. Some say that Scripture gives principles only and these must be viewed in today's context—that commands laid down for first century churches and Christians are not necessarily binding on twentieth century Christians, because of the differences in conditions and cultures. (They sometimes say that the Bible is progressive, with a writer like Paul changing his mind as he "matured" in his relationships with women. They're strangely silent on the subject of the inspiration of Scripture—2 Timothy 3:16.)

Christian feminists seem to be upset most about the lack of opportunity to use their gifts, since they are not allowed to engage in public preaching. They think they are looked on with a patronizing air and discriminated against. They say that the Bible does not discriminate between men and women as far as spiritual gifts are concerned, and they're quite right in this. In the passages relating to spiritual gifts there is no gift specified as for men alone (see 1 Corinthians 12). But the Lord of the church does make a difference between men and women when it comes to the *use* of gifts in the gatherings of His people, and surely He has the right to do so. As we will be dealing with the subject of spiritual gifts in Lesson 12, we will leave further discussion until then.

Spokesmen for the Christian feminists are particularly bothered about the submission required of wives in the hierarchical marriage relationship. They object to male dominance. They say that submission is not Biblical, except that all Christians are to submit one to another. (They retain Ephesians 5:21, but reject verse 22!) They view the usual marriage relationship as a one-way street, with women doing all the giving in: women submitting, giving in to men, giving up their "rights." They call for equality in all areas of life, including marriage, business or professional life, and ministry in the church. This is evident in the current demand for the ordination of women.

A common argument of all the feminists is that boys and girls are *taught* their sex roles from babyhood; they are brainwashed into behaving like a boy (later a man) or a girl (later a woman). This teaching of sex roles, they say, is based on the old-fashioned view of the female as dainty, emotional, maternal, somewhat helpless in a man's world; while the male is the breadwinner, strong and superior, excelling in sports and mechanics and financial understanding. They say that this sex stereotyping is artificial. Is it? Do the real physiological differences have no effect?

"Liberty" is the watchword. Women must be liberated from sex stereotyping, from domination by men, from the typical housewifely role. They must realize their "potential" in every area of life. For this the Christian feminists claim Biblical support. They credit Paul (in spite of his "male chauvinist" ideas and Jewish upbringing) with promoting the idea of unisex—"There is neither male nor female: for ye are all one in Christ Jesus" (Galatians 3:28).

Was it likely that Paul "changed his mind" (as some say), writing one thing in one letter and something else in another? Or did he write under the control of the Holy Spirit? Are the feminists picking and choosing among Paul's statements—"These we will accept; these we reject"? What authority does anyone have to sit in judgment on God's Word, deciding what is from God and what is just from Paul? Unless the Bible is authoritative—all of it—we have *no* authority on which to base our lives. A careful consideration *in their context* of the verses used by the feminists leaves us in no doubt that Paul was consistent in his teaching and that what he wrote was the word of the

Lord (1 Corinthians 14:37).

Christian liberation is that freedom known by the woman who accepts the Bible (all of it) as God's Word and seeks to follow God's commands to the letter. True liberty is the result of obedience. We have no right to question God's commands—no right to put a question mark where God places a period.

A Chinese proverb tells of two men walking along a river bank who saw a particularly lovely tree. One of the men sadly remarked that the poor tree was unable to move from that spot. Surely such a tree should be free! So they pulled it up to set it free! The point is obvious. The tree was free and beautiful in its appointed place, but dead afterwards. So are we free—joyously free—when we follow God's plan and accept the role He has assigned to us. As long as the train remains on the tracks, it is free to function effectively. As long as the sailboat obeys the law of the winds, it remains gloriously free.

So it is with men and women. God in His wisdom has appointed man as head, and woman as his complement and helper. He has assigned—and designed—the roles appropriate to each. And He has fitted us in every way to fill those roles with satisfaction. Would God, the wise and loving Creator, have planned for us anything that was not perfect? The secret of our fulfillment lies in acceptance of God's plan. The satisfied heart knows true freedom.

Does this mean non-creativity for the woman? Does it mean confinement to home chores? A door-mat complex? No! Our previous lessons dealing with both Old Testament and New Testament women demonstrate that women's ministry is not confined to the home (see Proverbs 31). And for the woman who waits on God, who listens and obeys, there is satisfaction beyond measure, even in the most difficult and seemingly limited circumstances. How could opening ourselves to the infinite, eternal Creator-God bring us into an experience that is narrow and barren? The woman who seeks to please God, who delights to do His will, whose life is focused upon God and not on herself, will find that He gives her the desires of her heart (Psalm 37:4).

Seeking self-fulfillment *for its own sake* leads inevitably to a barren and lonely selfishness. The way to real happiness and fulfillment is not self-seeking, but self-giving in love.

FURTHER STUDY

Read "Let Me Be A Woman." (Refer to the bibliography at the end of the course for details.)

When you have mastered this lesson, take the first part of Exam 6 (covering Lesson 11), questions 1-10 on pages 121-123 (right after Lesson 12).

LESSON 11

PERSONAL QUESTIONS TO PONDER

(Write out your answers to these questions. You may, if you wish, submit your answers to your instructor for comment and evaluation.)

1) Do I weigh the statements of Christian feminists in light of the teaching and tenor of God's Word?

_____

_____

_____

_____

2) In my experience, which kind of attitude has brought me more joy—self-seeking or loving self-giving?

_____

_____

_____

_____

Pray that God will help you weigh the statements of Christian feminists in the light of God's Word; that you will develop those kinds of attitudes that will make you a woman who pleases God.

MY PERSONAL PRAYER

_____

_____

Spiritual Gifts
(Romans 12:4-8; 1 Corinthians 12:7-11 and 27-31;
Ephesians 4:7, 8, 11-13)

Which of the gifts of the Spirit are for men? Which are for women? A study of this subject shows that *none* of the gifts was designated for one sex only. As we examine the gifts, bear in mind that any one of them may be your own!

DEFINITION

A spiritual gift is a notable capacity bestowed on a believer by God's grace for the edification, exhortation and comfort of God's people. The New Testament word for "gift" is *charisma,* taken from the Greek *charis* (meaning grace). In other words, these gifts are not of human origin but are freely given by God's grace, "as it hath pleased Him." They are bestowed "for the perfecting of the saints for the work of the ministry, for the edifying of the body of Christ" (Ephesians 4:11, 12). In other words, they are given for the purpose of *service,* not for private enjoyment.

DERIVATION

In the three major portions of Scripture dealing with gifts, we see each member of the Trinity mentioned as a source of gift. Romans

12:3—"... according as *God* hath dealt to every man the measure of faith." Ephesians 4:7—"Unto every one of us is given grace according to the measure of the gift of *Christ.*" 1 Corinthians 12:1, 11—"Concerning spiritual gifts ... all these worketh that one and the selfsame *Spirit,* dividing to every man severally as He will."

DESCRIPTION

Read carefully the following passages, listing the gifts as you read. Romans 12:4-8. 1 Corinthians 12:7-11, 27-31. Ephesians 4:7, 8, 11-13.

A convenient way of grouping the gifts, eliminating the overlapping in the passages, is to see them as *speaking* gifts, *serving* gifts, or *sign* gifts, as in the following arrangement.

A. Speaking gifts	B. Serving gifts	C. Sign gifts
apostles	helps	miracles
prophets	giving	healing
evangelists	government	tongues
shepherds/pastors	showing mercy	interpretation of
teachers	faith	tongues
exhorters	discernment	
word of knowledge		
word of wisdom		

A. Speaking gifts

1. Apostles—Apostleship can have both a general and a limited meaning. The word means "one who is sent," equivalent to our word missionary. In a general sense every Christian is a missionary, a person sent with a message. But in the special sense, the gift of apostleship was limited to the twelve disciples, who had been with Jesus from the beginning of His ministry, had had a personal call from Him, and had been witnesses of His resurrection. They laid the foundation of the church (Ephesians 2:20), had special authority, and were accredited by special signs. This special gift was necessary only in the earliest period of the church.

2. Prophets—This word also has a general sense and a limited sense. It means to speak or tell forth, and the preacher who

114

tells forth a message from God is a prophet. But the special gift of prophecy involved receiving a message from God *by special revelation* and declaring it. It was needed during the writing of the New Testament and was no longer needed when the books were completed, since God's entire message was then in written form and no new revelation could add to it.

3. Evangelists—This gift is the special ability to communicate the gospel clearly to unbelievers, with conversions resulting. This includes personal evangelism as well as public exercise. Apparently we can do the work of an evangelist even though we may not possess the special gift. See 2 Timothy 4:5.

4. Shepherds/pastors—These have a special ability to care for their fellow-believers—to guide, feed and guard them from evil, as a shepherd cares for his sheep.

5. Teachers—This gift involves a supernatural ability to explain clearly and apply effectively the truths of God's Word—not just imparting information, but leading others to the practice of Biblical precepts.

6. Exhorters—The exhorter comes alongside to urge a fellow-believer to pursue some course of conduct, or to encourage in view of failure or trial. He or she is a spiritual counsellor.

7. Word of knowledge—This gift enables the believer to search out and summarize the teachings of God's Word, to gain deep insight into divine truth, and to communicate it to others.

8. Word of wisdom—This gift involves the application of Biblical truths to the needs and problems of life, putting knowledge of the Word to work in daily experience.

B. Serving gifts

1. Helps—This gift enables one to serve faithfully behind the scenes, in practical ways assisting in the work of the Lord, encouraging and strengthening others spiritually as well. It would include the important ministry of prayer and also that of hospitality, which is highly regarded in the New Testament.

2. Giving—This is the God-given ability to give of one's self and

one's possessions to the Lord's work and to His people—sacrificially, wisely and cheerfully.

3. Government, or ruling—The one with this gift is able to set goals, to motivate others, to execute plans that promote the work of God and the welfare of His people.

4. Showing mercy—This is the Spirit-guided ability to show practical, compassionate love to sufferers in the body of Christ—not just a sympathetic word, but action involving a giving of oneself.

5. Faith—This, of course, is more than saving faith; it is the ability to see something that God wants to be done and to believe that God will do it even though it seems impossible. Those who have this gift "dream great dreams and tackle great tasks for God."

6. Discernment—Though every believer is responsible for discerning the spirits (1 John 4:1), some have a particular ability to do so—the ability to distinguish between the spirit of truth and the spirit of error: between what is of God and what pretends to be. This gift was especially needed before the completion of the New Testament.

C. Sign Gifts

1. Miracles—This gift involves the ability to do works of supernatural power, causing wonder, in order to confirm and authenticate the messenger and his message as being from God. This gift was necessary in the apostolic age.

2. Healing—This is the ability to heal any and all diseases by supernatural power. This seems to have been a temporary and confirmatory gift in the early days of the church.

3. Tongues and their interpretation—This involves the supernatural ability to speak in a language known by others which one has never learned. This, too, was characteristic of the apostolic age and was given to confirm the messenger and his message.

These three sign gifts differ from the other gifts in that nowhere

116

are we *commanded* to do them. There are no exhortations to do miracles, or healing, or to speak in tongues. But we are all expected to engage to some extent in evangelism (Mark 16:15), shepherding (Galatians 6:2, 10), teaching (Colossians 3:16), giving (1 Corinthians 16:2), etc., even though we don't have the particular gift involved.

DISCOVERY

How do I know which gifts I have? The best way is to try one. An honest effort, prayerfully exercised, can then be evaluated by these criteria: 1) Do I enjoy doing this? You *will* enjoy doing what God has gifted you for. 2) Do others confirm that I have this gift? Others can often evaluate your work better than you can yourself. Self-deception is all too easy. 3) Is it being used by God for His glory, in building up the body of Christ?

DEVELOPMENT

In a very practical way, it takes perseverance, diligence and hard work to develop a gift and to find opportunities to use it, but we are expected to use our gifts faithfully. "As every one hath received the gift, even so minister the same one to another, *as good stewards* of the manifold grace of God" (1 Peter 4:10). *"Neglect not* the gift that is in thee..." (1 Timothy 4:14). *"Stir up* the gift of God which is in thee..." (2 Timothy 1:6).

All the gifts given by the Head are needed for the proper building up and functioning of the body of Christ, even as the tiny piccolo plays its necessary part in a great orchestra and its absence would be noticed. It is the responsibility of all Christians, men and women alike, to exercise their gifts for the blessing and enrichment of one another.

"Yet," wrote the Apostle Paul, "show I unto you a more excellent" thing than the possession and use of gifts, and he pointed out the necessity of love (1 Corinthians 12:31—13:13). The exercise of gifts without love brings no blessing, but the believer who is walking in love to God and to fellow-Christians will be a channel of blessing to all around.

The quiet fruit of the Spirit (Galatians 5:22, 23) in a believer's life is of more value to God than the exercise of the most spectacular gifts. Therefore, we must be careful as we seek to discover and develop our spiritual gifts, not to get things out of balance—not to neglect the more important thing, the "more excellent way"—the way of love.

In the Introduction to this course we stated that we could have no higher honor than to *be* what God intended us to be. We have learned many lessons from this study of God's Word, but the simplest, yet most profound, statement of God's purpose for us—of what will please Him—is that we should be "conformed to the image of His Son" (Romans 8:29). It is the occupation of our heart with Christ and letting His Word dwell in us that produces His likeness in us. This is not gained by human effort or striving, but by yielding ourselves day by day to God. The Holy Spirit, working in a yielded life, produces in us likeness to our Lord and thus we become the kind of women who please God.

FURTHER STUDY

Read "The Dynamics of Spiritual Gifts." (Refer to the bibliography at the end of the course for details.)

When you are ready, complete Exam 6 by answering questions 11-20 on pages 123-124. (You should have already answered questions 1-10 as part of your study of Lesson 11.)

118

LESSON 12

PERSONAL QUESTIONS TO PONDER

(Write out your answers to these questions. You may, if you wish, submit your answers to your instructor for comment and evaluation.)

1) Have I identified my spiritual gift?

_____

_____

_____

_____

2) Am I using it for the benefit of the Lord's people?

_____

_____

_____

_____

3) Am I using it in love?

_____

_____

_____

_____

Pray that God will help you discover and develop your spiritual gift for the profit of others and that you will use it in love for His glory.

MY PERSONAL PRAYER

_____

_____

_____

_____

_____

_____

_____

THE WOMAN WHO PLEASES GOD

Exam
Grade _____

Name _____
(print plainly)

Address _____

City _____ State _____ Zip Code _____ Class Number _____

Instructor _____

LESSON 11

In the blank space in the right-hand margin write the letter of the correct answer. (50 points)

1. The early feminist movement had several concerns. Which of these was **NOT** included?
   a. abolition of slavery
   b. women's right to vote
   c. ordination of women
   d. equality with men in education   _____

2. Non-Christian feminists advocate
   a. Traditional-style marriage relationships
   b. egalitarian marriages
   c. different functions for husband and wife
   d. that even working wives should do all the home chores   _____

3. The Christian feminists say that
   a. they have no Scriptural backing for their position
   b. the Bible gives principles only, and they must be applied in today's context
   c. Paul was consistent in all his references to women
   d. they don't go along with the issues of the secular movement at all   _____

4. In regard to spiritual gifts, Christian feminists believe that
   a. men have different gifts than women
   b. men regard women's gifts with respect and admiration
   c. women have plenty of opportunities to use their gifts in the church
   d. women lack opportunity to use their gifts in the church   _____

121

5. Christian feminists say that the concept of a woman's submission to her husband is
   a.   not Biblical
   b.   helpful to the woman
   c.   harmful to the man
   d.   a two-way street _____

6. Feminists say that sex stereotyping
   a.   is artificial
   b.   is based on unquestionable facts
   c.   promotes the potential of women
   d.   is innate, not taught _____

7. According to some feminists, the Apostle Paul
   a.   denied the idea of unisex
   b.   was consistent in his remarks about women
   c.   was inspired by God in all he wrote
   d.   "matured" and changed his mind about women's role _____

8. The woman who knows true freedom is the one who
   a.   regards the whole Bible as God's Word
   b.   seeks to obey God's commands
   c.   accepts with gladness God's plan for her
   d.   does all of the above _____

9. The woman who accepts God's plan and seeks to do His will is
   a.   thereby confined to home chores
   b.   treated more like a doormat than a person
   c.   fulfilled and satisfied
   d.   stifled as far as creativity is concerned _____

10. We should seek self-fulfillment
   a.   as a worthwhile goal for its own sake
   b.   as an antidote to selfishness
   c.   through self-giving love
   d.   by following our own desires and interests _____

WHAT DO YOU SAY?

Have you found true freedom and fulfillment in acceptance of God's plan for you? Have you yielded to Him control of every area of your life?

_____

_____

_____

_____

_____

LESSON 12

In the blank space in the right-hand margin write the letter of the correct answer. (50 points)

11. A spiritual gift is
    a. a talent we are born with
    b. given for our own enjoyment
    c. given for the upbuilding of God's people
    d. given to very few Christians   _____

12. Spiritual gifts come to us from
    a. God the Father
    b. the Lord Jesus Christ
    c. the Holy Spirit
    d. all of the above   _____

13. Evangelism is a gift
    a. that was present only in apostolic times
    b. that could be used person-to-person
    c. that is meant to be used only in large campaigns
    d. that is used to help believers   _____

14. The gift of teaching
    a. is one that can be obtained through training
    b. is a relatively unimportant one today
    c. just means imparting information about God's Word
    d. should lead others to practice Biblical principles in their lives   _____

15. The ability to apply God's Word to the needs and problems of life is the gift of
    a. a word of wisdom
    b. a word of knowledge
    c. a prophet
    d. an apostle   _____

16. Which of the following would **NOT** be included in the gift of helps?
   a.   hospitality
   b.   prayer
   c.   preaching
   d.   cleaning the chapel _____

17. Government, or ruling, is a gift
   a.   that is given only to elders
   b.   that is given only to men
   c.   intended to promote the work of God effectively
   d.   for ordering others around _____

18. Which of the following was **NOT** a sign gift?
   a.   Giving
   b.   Healing
   c.   Working miracles
   d.   Speaking in tongues _____

19. I can be sure I have discovered my gift
   a.   even if I don't enjoy using it
   b.   even if others don't think so
   c.   if it makes me prominent in the church
   d.   if God is using it to build up His people _____

20. The possession of a gift
   a.   does not necessarily mean that I must use it
   b.   involves faithful use of it
   c.   is not granted to every believer
   d.   does not mean that it is needed _____

WHAT DO YOU SAY?

What spiritual gift has been given to you? Are you developing it and using it in love?

_____

_____

_____

_____

SUGGESTIONS FOR FURTHER READING

The Place of Women in the Church
  Charles C. Ryrie — Macmillan, New York

Let Me Be A Woman
  Elisabeth Elliot — Tyndale House, Wheaton

Life In His Body
  Gary Inrig — Harold Shaw Publishers

Hidden Art
  Edith Schaeffer — Tyndale House, Wheaton

The Dynamics of Spiritual Gifts
  William McRae — Zondervan, Grand Rapids

Obtain these books from, or order through, your nearest Christian bookstore.

EPILOGUE

This course has been designed to present in a positive way the characteristics of the woman who pleases God, and to help the student personally to move toward becoming this kind of woman. Is it possible that each one of us can become in life and character a person truly pleasing to God?

Many women would say, No. They have an inadequate self-concept—a mental image of themselves as being inferior—a bit of a failure—not able to measure up to others' accomplishments. Perhaps this feeling has been fostered in the church in the case of women who (wrongfully) view the matter of headship and submission as making them second class citizens. They go about feeling apologetic about themselves, afraid to try to do anything in case they fail. Failure would bring embarrassment and humiliation, so they play it safe and do nothing.

This lack of self-confidence is a serious matter. Henry Ford once said, "A person's mental picture of himself, more than any other factor, sets the ultimate boundaries of his achievements." It also keeps one anxious, uncertain, ineffective and uncomfortable in many situations.

The answer to this problem is the establishing and recognizing of the spiritual dimension of life. Do you feel inferior, of little value or account? Remember *God* loves you—unconditionally, just as you are—you're of value to Him (John 3:16; 1 John 4:9, 10). He loved you so much that He gave His Son to die for you, so that your sins might be forgiven and that you might become His child. If you have asked the Lord Jesus to be your Savior, then you *are* God's child (John 1:12). God has accepted you—you belong to Him (Ephesians 1:6). Does that not give you uplift in your self-concept? Second, remember that, now you are God's child, *He* is at work in your life to make you into a woman who pleases Him (Philippians 2:13). Is He likely to fail? (Philippians 1:6). Do you still feel inadequate to meet and cope with life situations? Then remember that the Lord is with you *at all times* to equip you for "every good work" (2 Corinthians 9:8). You don't face life alone—you have the Spirit of God dwelling within you (John 14:16, 17). Is *He* adequate for every situation? Conscious of His presence and yielded to Him, you can be adequate also.

We must, however, state once again that if you have not received Christ, you are *not* God's child. You have not been born into His family, for new birth comes by faith in Christ (Galatians 3:26). And if you have not accepted the Savior that God has provided, then there is no way for you to be the kind of woman who pleases God. You cannot count on His help or presence with you—you face life alone, relying on your own resources.

Someone has defined "peace" as "the conscious possession of adequate resources." Our resources in Christ cannot be estimated or imagined (Ephesians 1:19, 20; 3:20). The inner peace this gives us enables us to get our eyes off ourselves and to get away from preoccupation with the impression we may be making on others. From our position of inner peace and security, resting on the Lord, we find we're not so afraid of people—not so vulnerable—and we can begin to have a genuine care and concern for the welfare and happiness of others. We can love because we know we are loved (1 John 4:19). And our interest and caring for others can help them to affirm *their* self-concept. Goethe wrote, "Treat people as if they were what they ought to be, and you help them to become what they are capable of being." This is how God deals with us. He sees us, not as the faltering, sinning beings we are, but "in Christ," His Beloved—He sees us as we shall be, conformed to the image of His Son (1 John 3:2).

Is it right for you still to say, Yes, *but...?* (I'm not attractive, I don't know what to say to people, I'm not really good at anything, I don't have enough education, I have a physical handicap, etc.). Your problem then is that you're not willing to *accept* the way God has made you and the circumstances in which He has placed you. *He* has made you and has put you there—for His own good purpose. Don't be occupied with your own weaknesses and shortcomings—God knows all about them. *Yet* He has a plan and purpose for your life. Realize your worth in God's sight. Look at yourself as He does. Accept His evaluation, not your own, or society's. God has chosen you, loved you, bought you at tremendous cost because you're important and valuable to Him. Look to Him, seek His will and enabling, and you will be filled with praise as you see what He is able to do in you and through you. "As for God, His way is perfect ... it is God that maketh *my* way perfect" (Psalm 18:30-32).